Stalked by The Grim Reaper.

Mike Youngman.

There is more freedom out there in the wilderness than civilisation, just Mother Nature making the rules you cross her at your peril. The more I think about it the more I believe that the bubble of civilisation will one day burst, and Mother Nature will wipe out the virus that is infecting her domain! Mankind is the only one of Mother Nature's creations that takes what it wants from the her but is unwilling to adapt to an ever-evolving environment i.e. planet Earth instead he tries to change the environment to suit himself, selfishly ignoring the consequences on the rest of nature. She will take restitution.

"Mother Nature will take it all back"

Published in 2020 by FeedARead.com Publishing

First Edition

A CIP catalogue record for this title is available from the British
Library.

Chapter One

I had a very strict father as an army officer he had to keep up the appearance of control at all times which was easy with my 3 sisters, but I was a different matter altogether. At thirteen, I was constantly in trouble for coming home late, I suffered the wrath of an angry officer as opposed to an angry father. 1964 Dad was posted to Malaysia, a little later the family followed, it was heaven to me, the thick jungle and long sandy beaches it was hot and sticky, I soon acclimatised, I ran wild for years camping out in the jungle. My Malayan friend Chris the wog as he liked to be known, he taught me the ways of the jungle we spent many a weekend swimming out to the dreaded bat island, some 500 yards out from the beach it was very hazardous, the sea was teeming with large jellyfish and the odd shark. One evening as I was sat on the beach by the fire, a soldier walked by arm in arm with a young Chinese woman. The next morning as I ran into the sea for my morning wash, something hairy became entangled around my hand, as I pulled free I could see to my horror, it was the half eaten face of the young Chinese woman I saw with the soldier the previous night, once I got the body on the beach I could see her head it was bashed in, I felt quite sick, sea lice covered her head, they were feeding on the blood. I ran back to the Army base and reported it. Sometime later the soldier was sent back to Australia for trial. A few weeks later the soldiers wife attempted revenge by accusing me of breaking into her home and attempting to rape her, lucky for me, (a 14 year old at the time) the evening it was alleged to have occurred it just so happened I had arrived home the same time as my father, two hours before the alleged crime had taken place, dad being the strict military type soon had it all under control, so my alibi was good but still, Dad was livid with me, he had to explain to his commander, how his son came to be involved in this sort of incident and why was a young lad of my young age out at this time of night, and camping alone. He was advised to get me under control and to stop me running wild throughout the base and the surrounding jungle, there were so many reports of trouble and I was frequently mentioned in a number of incidents that had occurred. So, my father kept me occupied I spent time sweeping up spent bullet shells at the Army shooting range. I lost count of the canings I received at school the headmaster pleaded with my parents to calm me down, so you can see I was a bit of a wild child. The school in an effort to teach us responsibility had its own small zoo, it consisted of five small monkeys, several monitor lizards, a large Avery which consisted of minor birds and parrots and other species. There were several snakes including four pythons, and a pair of rather nasty looking Pit Vipers, who lashed out at anyone who looked near the tank, we nicknamed them Jekyll &Hyde. It seemed cruel to me to have wild animals restricted this way after all I knew how they must feel being wild myself, so I released them all one evening after school this caused a riot on the nearby housing estate, some houses had to be evacuated until the snakes and Monitor lizards were removed by the army, so once again dad had to come up with an explanation for the Commander, at least we all had a week off school until the school was deemed safe once the animals were accounted for, apart from the pair of Pit vipers Jekyll & Hyde, they were never found. I was the first to be interrogated and found guilty by reputation, I did admit it in the end I was just a kid what could they do. Expel me from school and a good beating from Dad. I was used to that he was a bit of a bully I had them quite regularly anyway, like all army barmy types "it's his way" Mum told me it did not make me feel any better. So that is my wild side it has stuck with me throughout my life and may help understand why my life was so eventful. There were times when I feared for my life, I ask myself "what the hell am I doing" But I just thought of a 9 to 5 job! No thanks.

1977, Dad started working in Iran he took Mum and my three Sisters, I was left living in my father's empty house by that I mean not even carpets or curtains. I had completed a Toolmaker apprenticeship and got paid off soon as it was complete, I had no idea what I was to do with my life. I had no encouragement or financial help from my father. I received a pittance from the dole, which was not enough to get by on, let alone find a job! Why do they call it "job seekers allowance"?

At 24 I was just a drop out aimless as was my eccentric mate Neil. Neil was extremely intelligent; maths came very easily to him he could calculate most formulas in his head within minutes. Everyday life was a mammoth task for him he didn't consider them important enough to distract him from the question "why humans existed" , He had the looks of your local eccentric, the long dark bushy curly hair and full beard the intense stare from his dark brown eyes tended to put people on guard, he was actually a big softy he drove a 1962 Beetle that had a faulty starter which often jammed but only at critical moments the only cure was to rock the car in 1st gear by which time we'd become the entertainment for the local tarts posing outside the pub. "A laughingstock"! We often ended up pushing LS (little sod was the cars name) three miles back to his mums tiny flat by tiny I mean touch all four walls of the kitchen and bathroom with your arms outstretched. Neil slept on the very well-worn sofa. One Sunday morning, there was banging on the front door I was nursing a hangover from a skin full of Neil's home brew beer. I could hear Neil shouting at the top his of voice

"Mike get up and open the door"

I'd got used to lying in, since I had no future as far as I was concerned, I did finally open the door to a frantic Neil ranting on about the oil boom in Aberdeen and how an exciting future awaited us.

"get packed get packed" he was wailing

"we need to leave now it's a 6-hour drive"

he frowned and looked at his car "maybe 8 in this car"

He carried on about how his amazing mother had made us a picnic for the journey. I had no clue about the oil industry at all neither did Neil

"it's madness" I told him.

Neil shouted

"What have we got to lose? Mike our lives are going nowhere"

,

"good point mate" I said there's nothing to keep me here, I thought. I threw some clothes in a bag and we left in high spirits Neil having told me of the mega money they were paying on the oil rigs. By the time we reached Lancaster my imagination had run wild, I had bought my new motorcycle and was off on holiday to the Grand Canyon, at which point I was brought back to reality feeling the car slowing down to a stop on the hard shoulder on the m6. A puncture, not serious we changed it in quick time and continued on our speedy journey at 60 mph this was the maximum safe speed the old beetle would go before the car started shaking quite wildly so 60 mph it was all the way to Aberdeen, it started snowing shortly after Carlisle, so 60 mph then became 40 mph. A Marathon drive of eight hours brought us into Aberdeen exhausted, we slept in the car for a few hours,

Neil poked me "wake up Mike look"

The site of a man beating a woman was my first experience of Scotland, the woman was on her knees blood was running over the pavement, we both leapt from the car, Neil grabbed the man while I helped the woman to her feet. Then the strangest thing happened the woman started beating up on me and screaming

"leave him leave him you bastard."

She broke free and threw a punch which nearly knocked me off my feet

"fuck this Neil leave them to it"

Neil laughed "you're going to have a real shiner their Mike".

The love birds walked off holding hands this stayed with me for years after Scottish men were mean to their wives yet (here's the confusing bit) their wives adore them?

"This is not normal Neil they both covered in blood trying to kill each other now back in love is this normal in Scotland".

Who knows Mike? anyway we need to go find East Tullos trading estate"

Driving into the city centre we were clearly lost so it was time for a rethink like, buy a map perhaps? Neil was determined to manage so I asked this fella for directions to East Tullos industrial estate I should have known better. I couldn't understand a single word the man said all, errs and words without a break in between, I never stood a chance, so I politely thanked him, we drove on. Starving hungry we stopped at the first chip shop where we obtained the directions to the industrial estate that Pam, Neil's mum had insisted this was the hub of operations for the North Sea oil industry in fact there were only 4 companies on this estate

one of which, to our amazement offered us Roustabout(labour) jobs right way, the only question he asked us was
"Are you guys aware the job will involve a lot of manual labour"
"I always thought Manual labour was a Mexican" Laughed Neil.
The manager a French Canadian had a quick laugh then frowned at Neil. Then he just asked if we could leave for Sumburgh the next day which really caught us wrong footed I just thought he was testing our resolve, so I just said
"of course, we can"
We signed, employment contract even though the last paragraph stated.
"The company reserves the right to change the conditions of this contract without notice."
So, the contract meant nothing, he sent us off to their company B&B, we would be picked up the next morning at 7 am. The B&B happened to be opposite a pub/hotel called the Malacca, so we checked in and along with the Hard hats we'd been issued posed in the bar like two hard case oil men. The place was full of desperate idiots just like us all thinking the big money was or most in our grasp. Our imaginations were running wild. I laugh about it now knowing how we must have looked, when informed by some real oil men the truth about the living conditions on board the rigs i.e. no doors on the toilets or showers 6 men to a room, and working 12 hour shifts only having 30 minutes for dinner and two 15 minute breaks a day, and no stopping work even for rain or snow.
" No doors on the toilets I can't believe that" I exclaimed,
A Canadian told me it was so you couldn't skive off work he chuckled,
"one's trips to the bog were monitored, a lot of guys were just taking the piss!"
 (Pardon the pun) it was a chance for a well-deserved rest legal or not as we found out later.
I turned to face Neil "This was all your idea Neil we'll never survive it; it's gonna be murder."
The Canadian laughed "it's no holiday lads you will earn your bucks the pay is good for a reason,"
 he frowned "it is very hard work and dangerous so good luck boys".
We left the bar expecting to last a day or so before getting the sack I felt very nervous now I never slept a wink that night. The next morning

brought another new terrifying prospect as I peeked outside the window what did I see the wind blowing snow against the window,

yes, a blizzard! "oh my god we are going to die" I sighed.

I told Neil I had decided to go home

"don't be stupid Mike you have nothing there so what have you got too loose?"

"but Neil I don't think I can do this rig work it sounds awful hard work"

"Mike look at some of these lads going with us some are real wimps skinny and pale faced you are well built thick set you will adapt believe me I wouldn't fight you"

Neil chuckled.

I was convinced the compliment did it, so along with all the other green hands the company rep herded us on to a bus for the airport my hands shaking with fear of the unknown, most of the lads including Neil were much bigger than me I knew I would not manage this I was scared to death at what lay ahead I felt sick.

A voice broke my thoughts of how I might die. "It could be a bit of a rough flight boys the weathers not good but no worries we have good pilots".

I felt the blood drain from my face it was a short drive to the airport. we boarded the plane with trepidation of what was to come. The Shetlands are a desolate place no trees very wind swept, the rep was right the weather had us bouncing all over the sky the landing was quite frightening the plane swayed all over the place before touching down with a mighty thud, I was expecting to see a pair of wheels come up through the floor of the plane. After collecting our bags, we sat through a safety video instruction of how to survive in the sea if you end up in it. It seemed clear to me your chances were remote at best, it continued about working on Rigs and about all the hazards of working on an oil rig. All this was giving me grave doubts whether I could do this. After the video we were told to don a thin plastic suit (survival suit) which would protect us for up to four minutes in a rough sea

"what's the fucking point" I heard my voice beam out,

the rep gave me a real dirty look, the other suckers just laughed feeling sick and fighting the urge to run out the door they announced that there was a delay to wait and see if the weather would improve so we sat for 5 hours. The powers that be decided we should chance it because it was getting dark, we could always turn back if necessary, Neil looked scared too his face had paled, and his smile vanished.

I shrugged my shoulders "what the fuck."

I donned the suit before we were led out the door into the blizzard it was worse than ever, I could hardly make out the helicopter through the driving snow which stung my face. The rep instructed us to keep hold of a rope which had been attached to the Chopper it was there to help us find the chopper through the blizzard and high wind it was made worse by the down draught from the roaring chopper blades. I fought my way up the short steps into the Helicopter I strapped myself into the seat next to Neil I could feel the chopper sway back and forth under the attack of the blizzard. Once strapped in with our life jackets on the pilot warned us of the imminent bumpy flight that lay ahead, this really spooked me,

I nervously shouted over the chopper engine roar into Neil's ear "Neil they won't mind if we get off and go home will they."

He smiled and shook his head meaning "yes they would" then rolled his eyes as if to say, "Mike you idiot."

I squeezed my hands together for comfort I could not let anyone see the fear written all over my face when a sudden great surge thrust me upwards pressing me in to my seat upwards we soared until we were swallowed into the blizzard the ground vanished in seconds, I could feel my body compressed into the seat. I was scared shitless I had no idea what I was getting into or where I was going, my mind raced all the possible outcomes of this folly rushed through my head. I would never forgive Neil if I died! Little did I know that was the first day of a thirty-year career filled with adventures, and life-threatening incidents, journeys into the unknown I saw things many people would never see, I nearly lost my life on several incidents. I often wonder where I would be now had I quit that terrifying first day.

The North Sea during the seventies and eighties was a rough and dangerous place to work, 80-foot waves were common as are the 100mph winds, but you carried on working regardless of this. "Hurry up." was all you heard.

There was no let-up we had to keep working for 12 hours a day every day, the men who worked the North sea at that time must have been some of the fittest men in the world especially if you worked in the drilling section like I did. I know I've never been as fit as I was then, my muscles burned every day my legs ached from running up and down several flights of stairs often ten times a day, swinging sledgehammers until your arms turned to jelly, needless to say safety was a second

9

thought the amount of men with 4 fingered hands was common place. Fortunately, having witnessed my share of these finger loss incidents, I took great precaution to ensure I remained with all ten fingers despite using the evil spinning chain for 3 years.

The spinning chain was used to screw one drill pipe in to another (normally 6" DIA 30/40 feet long) in simple terms once wrapped around the pipe several times it was a tug of war between the roughneck and the 500 ton winch pulling it, once the pipe was tight the chain tended to jump under the operators fingers if you were not positioned right the chain coils tighten on your gloves and dragged your fingers into the ever tightening chain crushing the operator's fingers into jam. I had a number of horrifying experiences on a number of incidents where I was convinced the grim reaper was hovering over my shoulder. On one particular incident we were 15 minutes into our one hour chopper flight from Sumburgh to the Brent Delta platform it was partly foggy I was sat next to Neil half asleep, I jumped awake the chopper, swung over onto its side and plummeted downwards to the north sea it would swallow us up, down the chopper fell at a terrifying rate my body strained at the seat belt the blood drained from my face my arse was having a hot flush! I managed a quick glance at the others who looked deathly pale I grabbed Neil and told him what a great mate he had been
"I love you pal" I squeaked out,

I thought he should know before the end came, as the raging North Sea filled the window grey with white streaks which meant it was rough down there ever faster, we plunged through the snow,

Thoughts rushed through my mind "how will I die will it be the impact or maybe I will drown or even just freeze to death,

"please god I hope you are watching don't let me suffer too much I've been a good person,"

(I actually never believed but I did for that moment) I found it interesting how when in these sort of situations, one's first instinct is to grab the person nearest to you and your thoughts run through the mind at a hundred miles an hour. Suddenly the sound of the motors changed like they were at maximum the rotor blades made a clapping sound as they tried to bite into the air, we started slowing down our descent slowed to a hover over a raging sea, not a 100 ft. below us I was brought back to the here and now by Neil shrugged me off

"Mike let go of my arm your hurting me you idiot" "Sorry pal" I muttered.

It was then I could feel the sweat running down my face and neck, in fact, every part of my body was sweating I enquired

"Neil are you pouring with sweat"?

"fuck off Mike what's the matter with you" laughed Neil, with a quizzical frown "get a grip"

He was a cool customer his philosophy was if you know the inevitable why worry, easy to say. Our dive was halted seconds from impact by our very pale faced pilot he regained control of the Puma Helicopter just feet from the dark foreboding and angry North Sea the chopper remained motionless for what seemed an age with just the sound of the engines, in an eerie daze we all stared at each other two guys threw up, some had their head in their hands Neil and I just stared at each other in shock I couldn't help it

I shouted at the top of my voice "Fuck".

Once we landed on the Delta the hero pilot shut down the craft and told us how an RAF jaguar had missed us by the narrowest of margins the slip stream had taken the air from the chopper blades causing us to drop out of sky two days passed before my hands stopped trembling I know now why people use the expression

"I shit myself" because I very nearly did.

later that trip Neil called me over,

"Mike what was that you said during the incident on the chopper I couldn't quite make out what you said," of course, I lied.

"I just wondered if you were ok,"

He gave me a puzzled look

"I am sure it was something like, "you pal"

"hmm can't say don't remember" I mumbled. A letter of apology was received from the RAF a week later and displayed on the rig notice board. All this ruined my plan to pursue a skydiving career!! Several trips later I was promoted to motorman an oil field term for assistant Mechanic the last sucker had been badly burned by hot oil while working on one of the very large engines. This day the Tool pusher shouted to me across the deck

"Mike, I hear you know about engines,"

I could not wait for an opportunity to get away from the cold wet and windy deck so hastily I blurted

"yes of course"

"get your arse down to the engine room Mike it will be more money an easier job, but you will need to do another 2 weeks."

11

That was the drawback, plus I would be on opposite shift to Neil! More money! Hell, how could I lose? I located the engine room opening the engine room door three huge engines filled my view, twenty feet long perhaps seven feet high the noise level was overpowering, I could not enter the room the noise was like an impenetrable barrier, I released the door it slid shut on its own I felt a hand on my shoulder, I looked around there stood the chief Mechanic yet another Canadian.

"Hey Buddy, what are you doing in there?"

"I'm the new motor man" I replied

"Ok come with me I will show you around what's your name"

"Mike" I replied

"My name is Ron I am the boss for this area I 'll be training you Mike."

We ascended the staircase into what's known as the switch room, signs everywhere danger 600 volts.

"600 volts wow that's a lot"

"you bet we need it, Mike, there's some mighty big machinery here I will be delegating you your work from now, on don't pay any attention to the Tool pushers they know nothing, just do what I tell you ok, the last thing we need is a blackout that's what happens if the engines stop there's no electricity which means no drilling, so the powers that be will want to know why and they will ask us first."

"Who looks after them then?" I asked

"You do Mike!"

I nearly stopped in my tracks I had never had such huge responsibility before, and I'd never seen engines like that before, it suddenly occurred to me maybe I had bitten off more than I could chew.

"It's my job to teach you Mike so we can start by fuelling up"

Ron handed me an empty five-gallon drum.

"This is where you start there is 5 remote welding units that require fuelling up about every 4 hours the diesel is here just open the valve and keep at it I suggest you top them all before lunch then you can take an hour any problems I'll be here"

He showed me the office and how to fill out the reports.

"ok. see you later I will show you the main engines."

So the marathon began least that's how it felt running around the platform with a 5 gallon drum filled with diesel topping up welding units and other small power units by the time I'd got around them all I had to start again, the hook up of the platform had not been completed yet, welders outnumbered us all. Welders have a fire watcher bit of a joke really this is usually someone who is no use to man or beast this person simply looks for a fire starting while the welder is at work, how utterly boring I once saw a fire watcher falling asleep standing up, flames were licking all around his ankles, he and the welder were completely unaware of it so I ran over and smothered the flames we all burst out laughing forgetting I was stood there with my drum full of diesel, feeling pleased with myself until the welder looked up and went berserk shouting at me

"get that diesel away from here you moron"

Ever felt a right Prat. Strangely the following trip a firefighting course was arranged for us, all hands were to participate before going offshore. The course required two men without any breathing aids running into an inferno contained in a two storey corrugated iron building the idea being to rescue a dummy of equal weight and size of an average man, once you had crawled through the 20foot tunnel then scrambled up the 10foot ladder and run along a 20 foot staging down the next ladder to find the dummy laying at the base, we knew it was there the instructor had told us, we ran in dived into the tunnel and crawled out the end climbed the ladder ran along the staging down the ladder laid down flat to see the dummy under the smoke, at this point your skin was burning as were your eyes my nose was running my lungs were coughing up crap so we left the dummy there, we ran back to the start passing the next suckers to enter the fire house we burst out laughing at the horrified faces as they watched us burst through the smoke filled building black with soot nose running eyes watering coughing our lungs up in the process. No one ever managed to rescue the dummy. One older contestant nearly did he had a heart attack at the finish line, another lad was violently sick he caught the next train home. The survival course was not so funny either, it involved the entire crew being squeezed into a lifeboat, sailed out of Aberdeen harbour left to drift, until someone was sick, of course, once it started, we were all sick. Believe me sea sickness is no joke all this made us a bit more aware of what it would be like in a fire offshore.

Crane drivers are the unsung heroes of the North Sea, they sit in a tiny cab 3ft by 4ft on the top of 30ft pedestal on the rig, unloading Boats 150 feet below them on a sea with a 60foot swell it was a very disconcerting feeling, Once a load is hooked on to the Crane it jerks forward toward the sea it moves a few inches under the stress of the load, so just for a couple of seconds it gives you a feeling of impending doom, not for the faint hearted.

I was a year into my new motorman's job and learning fast, I was on nights it was a normal North Sea night high winds and 60ft waves, I was servicing the East Crane the driver Dick turned up he squeezed past me.

"I am going to do a snatch lift its high priority." (one very fast lift)

"are you mad it's too rough Dick" I shouted over the engines

"Naa! it will be ok" Dick replied and started the winches.

"well I'm off back down to the deck then"

so off I scurried soon as I reached the deck I heard the crack of the crane boom wires snapping, I looked down at the boat far below as it pitched up and down like a cork, I could see the cranes load it had snagged on the boat, I watched as the Crane was systematically ripped from its foundations and the platform by the weight of the boat, the crane was engulfed in to the giant waves, just missing the boat it vanished leaving just the cable still entangled around the boat. All the deckhands stood about in shock looking down at the smashed-up supply boat and like me wondering where the hell was Dick? I broke the spell that had me in shock I ran around the base of the crane there was dick lying in a heap it was my first dead body!

I was dump founded at a loss my mind raced what should I do but I needn't have worried the Tool pusher and OIM arrived we stood in silence looking at Dicks body, the Medic arrived he rushed over to Dick to checked over him he looked up in shock "Dick's dead!"

I asked myself "what if?"

We had a Tool pusher called Ray Egginburger can you believe that true none the less that was his name. When I was on night shift most of the time, he would often call me over to the office for a game of chess, every time I opened the door to the office the first thing, he'd say in a loud strong voice was,

"Mike do you believe in the living bible"

every time like it was procedure and every time, I told him.

"no Ray why"

so, Ray told me like it was his discovery

"you can't trust women the bible refers to them as serpents it was Eve who persuaded Adam to eat the apple so god decided as punishment all women will suffer during childbirth no other animal on this planet does just women, didn't you know that Mike"

"Really I didn't but I do now Ray"

Ray had the chess board all set up so, he made the first move followed by the same sequence of moves, he used every game I could have beaten him in a few moves, I let him win just so I could get away for breakfast, followed by Ray five minutes later, he would proudly announce his victory by shouting across the busy galley

"hey, beat you again Mike"

He finally lost his marbles one evening he locked himself out of his office so he climbed up through the roof panels intending to gain access to his office, but he became disorientated and took a wrong turn and fell through the false ceiling onto the desk of the OIM, the OIM was not amused he was reading as this body crashed on to his desk not inches from his face, he dived for cover knocking over his coffee machine which in turn spilt coffee and water all over his copier he dashed from his office looking very pale he nearly had a heart attack he looked back, moments later came to his senses he shouted very angrily at Ray.

"Fuck sake man, go and see the medic right now and stay there"

Last I heard, Ray was sent ashore deemed mentally unstable by the rig medic. Once back in Aberdeen rumour had it that Eginburger became convinced his wife had been unfaithful. they had an argument, she drove off, he pursued her in his car her across Aberdeen forcing her off the road, she ran in to a bank hoping to hide from this raging nut case he caught up with her in the bank on Union street, he held her securely in a headlock he tried to convince the bank security guard to help him beat her up,

Diagnosed as insane he was deported then subsequently committed once he reached the States.

July 1979 a very sad day, a crew on board a flight from Sumburgh to Aberdeen went off the end of the runway into the sea, I lost some great work colleagues that day I was lucky, I never made the flight I gave up my seat so someone more important could make a meeting in Aberdeen. Neil could not carry on after that very sad day he quit working offshore.

1982, I was working for Bawden drilling a Canadian company owned by Mr. Peter Bawden who treated his drilling crews as if we were his

15

boys, he would wait for the crews arriving back at Aberdeen airport then take us all to one side, ask us how our trip went and would we all be coming back again next trip? Such was the turnover of personnel in the North Sea it was a very dangerous job at that time. Smiling at all his boys Peter would hand out the pay cheques plus a gift like a Zippo lighter or puma pocketknife, he always seemed genuinely pleased to see us return without injuries. After a couple of years, I got the chance to try my hand at working the Derrick

"not for the faint-hearted"

I had been warned the derrick hand spends his day standing on a small platform 3 ft. wide by 7ft long so you could walk out to the centre of the Derrick, a 100ft up, heaving pipe out into the centre of the derrick directly into the pipe elevators, then close them around the pipe as they passed me at by at speed all this would be carried out in one motion leaving the derrick man leaning out from his monkey board at 45 degrees his harness taking his weight. I got the hang of it for about a year, it was such hard work tripping the pipe as they called it until that day came! It was really windy the blocks were swinging about I had a short pipe so I dropped to my chest and heaved the pipe out to the passing elevators, but the elevators swung towards me the handles struck me in the face knocking me out, I rolled over the side and plunged toward the rig floor 100ft below, luckily the safety harness I wore reached the end of its slack and stopped my fall instantly crushing my ribs, lucky for me I was unconscious I awoke in the hospital, one rib was pressing on my lung which made breathing extremely painful. It was a long time before I could return to work My Derrick man's days were over, I hated it anyway I was a bit too small for the job anyway most derrick hands are big strong lads, pulling pipe is hard work. I later managed to get another motorman's Position (assistant Mechanic). It was a sad day when Peter Bawden decided to sell his company because he wanted to get into Politics,

In Canada apparently if you are in Politics you cannot have any other incomes or jobs, Common sense I'd say, unlike the UK where Politicians can have any amount of jobs earning themselves huge incomes I call this a conflict of interest, and very greedy or perhaps its laws for them and laws for the public(corruption). Noble drilling bought the company.

I worked for Noble ending up on the Piper Alpha and sometimes on the Claymore platform which was crewed mainly with nut cases the chief Mechanic on the Piper for one, he was a big strong man about 6ft 4" his face wore a permanent scowl like he was pissed off, if you looked him in the eye he would bark at you

"yes, what's your problem?"

so needless to say, you had to be very guarded what you said he was easily stressed up and everyone knew it they played on it and often to their regret.

This day I was sat in the coffee shop with him when a roughneck came in looked at Dougie

"ah Dougie I needed to strip a tool in the workshop, but your bench was covered in hydraulic bits, so I chucked them all in a box out of my way ok."

I knew what was about happen earlier on that morning Dougie had carefully stripped the hydraulic pump and meticulously laid the parts out in order on the bench, he had a really bad temper, I could see colour of his face turn a furious red the lips tightened he sprung to his feet and leapt all of 20 feet across the room and grabbed the roughneck by the throat then pinned him to the floor,

"you bastard Ill rip your fucking head off sonny"

the roughneck pleaded "no no I am just kidding,"

but the strong hands of the chief must have tightened even more he could no longer talk Dougie pressed his knee down hard into the chest of the roughneck, everyone in the coffee shop froze in shock at the vicious attack, I realised the roughneck was actually suffocating, grabbing the chief I tried to pull him off it took 3 of us to prize them apart, the roughneck was deathly pale he spoke with a croak

"you're a mad bastard you were going to kill me,"

Dougie stared angrily at the roughneck,

"Never try that wind up shit with me sonny next time I will kill you now fuck off"

Dougie still trembled with rage his hands and lips still trembled he looked directly at me, then pushed his finger into my chest.

"Mike don't ever cross me, I have a terrible temper and this job is stressing me out, and Mike! Never interfere again right"

He meant it too

"you would have killed him if I hadn't and you would be in real trouble then"

"I don t care no one messes with me right"

Dougie's eyes bored a hole right through me he meant it alright. He stormed off across the deck shoving a roustabout out of his way as he went, he was a man with serious issues something was eating at him, unfortunately he was later killed on Piper Alfa.

One other chief Mechanic who worked on the claymore platform would hide so he could watch the workshop door thinking the tool pushers were spying on him sniper style, the day I started on that platform I was waiting outside the workshop door so I could report to him, I heard a whisper from behind a large round tank.

"Are you Mike"

I looked around

I whispered back,

"where are you?"

"over here" he whispered

I spotted him peeking from behind a storage tank, so I went over.

"We're being watched you know but I've got this"

he showed me the 2foot length of 1-inch steel pipe he held tightly in his fist, I wasn't sure what to say so I blurted out

"let's get a cuppa and talk about it"

"Cuppa tea! The cure for all problems in the entire UK, he shouted,

"No, I need to watch over the workshop, to catch the pusher eye balling the workshop,"

(another one succumbed to the pressure I thought just like Egginburger).

I reported the incident to the medic, the nut case was flown off the platform. It turned out the Mechanic would not leave his position behind the tank he even slept there. I'm sure he was committed just like Egginburger.

While at home on the 3rd July I received a call from the office asking if I would return early and do a trip on Piper Alpha, their mechanic was sick, I told them I could not come back so soon! To my horror on the news, I heard of the disaster this was the 6 of July, I lost a lot of friends that day especially my very good friend Les Morris, the

Canadian, tool pusher, I guarantee you will never meet a better human being, Les was a father of eight children he never stopped talking about them.

The story was, he found a way off the burning platform through the flames, down a bulk hose he ran back to the galley to tell the people gathered at their muster points, but the muster checker would not allow anyone to leave he told Les that choppers were coming, Les tried in vain to convince him it would not happen, one roustabout who will remain nameless went with him sadly Les was killed by the next explosion while he was in the sea. The roustabout told me all about it from his wheelchair at the memorial.

Is there a god? I don t think so If there is how does he justify allowing the good to die so young. Ask a Vicar he will just tell you God works in mysterious ways, they say you must have faith, but faith has to be earned how has God earned his by a book! I along with six other Bawden hands worked with Red Adair's men extinguishing the remaining small fires on the wreck of the Piper. I continued my position as Mechanic on the Claymore Platform. One of the consequences after the Piper incident was all the Turbine generators had to be run on diesel because the gas had been shut down until the Cullen report was complete, Every 3rd day a boat tied up and I had to lift 24 large steel hatches about 2 meters by 2 meters about 20mm thick and very heavy, however once that was complete 24 fuel valves had to be opened. My tool pusher at the time was a very kind man he came to me one day watched me heaving these large hatches off.

"Mike you need assistance this is a hard job I will arrange to get you someone big and strong"
spoken in a strong Swedish accent by Chris the 7-foot Tool pusher.

"Right Ok Chris"
half an hour later a I heard a powerful voice calling,
"Mike the Mechanic, where are you?"
"I Stuck my head above the hatch to see this lad even taller than Chris the pusher he must have been 7ft plus he reached down to me with this enormous hand and lifted me out of the hatchway like I was nothing.
"So, have you been sent to help me?"
I asked him in nervously. In a Liverpool accent he replied

"Yeah I have, call me Shaun let me do all the heavy lifting that's all I am good for"

"I am sure that's not true Shaun we need to open all these valves"

I told him, Shaun insisted I wait for him to do it because he did not need to climb into the hole to operate the valves he just bent down his giant hands which covered the valve wheel completely and effortlessly opened each of the 24 valves. My other assistant was Ted the motorman a slightly effeminate man and very clever, I'm sure he could talk his way out of a murder even if he was caught red-handed, on first impressions he came across as a mummy's boy even at the age of 52 and single with a 28 year old girlfriend, he had the gift of the gab the thick wavy hair combed tightly back from his cheeky looking face he always looked as if he was about start laughing and yes he was great fun to work with. Ted was a very intelligent man who regularly completed the time's crossword inside 30 minutes, the posh voice threw you at first, but it inevitably led to some smart remark at some body's embarrassment, it helped the two-week trip fly. Laughing as he approached us through the enormous warehouse, "Hey Mike, do you know the hulk is stood behind you," he was referring to Shaun,

"where the hell did you find him Frankenstein's cabin no more lifting gear for us then we just keep him with us Laughed Ted "Ask him to carry my bags up to the helideck when I am leaving will you."

Ted's laughing faded away as Shaun gave him a piercing stare then took a few steps closer the colour drained from Ted's face he looked like a ghost, It was Shaun's turn for a laugh, the look of relief on Ted's face was priceless when a grin emerged over Shaun's face, "It's ok mate any friend of Mikes you know what I mean Mike treats me with respect you do the same and we'll be fine what's your name?"

Teddy or Ted," Ted nervously quipped, Shaun laughed, Ted was clearly relieved by Shaun's comments it was only then I could see how big Shaun was, Ted and I barely came up to his chest he truly was the tallest human being I'd ever seen, he shook Ted's hand it was like shaking hands with a baby yes, he was one huge lad alright.

The engine room on the Claymore was vast, there was a good six foot wide walkway in between the three large engines which spanned ten feet high and twenty-five feet long one could see down the full length of the room to the windows of the switch room, I was servicing number two engine, I could see Ted through the window sat at the desk in the switch room reading the paper, his feet up on the desk the lazy sod,

"just shout if you need me Mike Iv a head ach, I'll go for a sit down for 5 minutes besides you v got the hulk to help you,"
 Laughed Ted.

 So, there he was sat at the desk in the switch room, the door open in walked the rig manager! Terry, he was a strong disciplinarian kind of man a head down and arse up believer, but a popular leader he looked after his boys, he made a beeline for Ted who was still sat at the desk with his head buried in the paper, feet on the desk oblivious to Terry's approach it was like a silent movie as the manager stood glowering over Ted, but Ted never flinched he calmly folded the paper to his chest smiled at Terry a short chat ensued, then Terry left, Ted just beamed a smiled at me then carried on reading the paper.

"I bet he's been fired," was my first thought.

I rushed through the soundproof door,

"Ted what did he say did he fire you?"

"No, I asked him to help me with 10 across but he couldn't then he left" laughed Ted,

I once ask Ted why he was content with his lot as a motorman.

"Mike once your promoted to Mechanic you have responsibility, with that you get accountability, no thanks to much hassle, if I screw up the chief just thinks it's me, stupid Ted the motorman, if I was mechanic like you Mike I'd be up in front of the OIM and possibly fired, this is easy for me why to spoil it."

Fair enough I thought there's no answer to that, Ted continued,

"there's a long queue of folk ready to take our jobs tomorrow, so we're easily replaced, Mike, for you and me it's a piece of cake so make the most of it while it's good".

He spoke too soon, what transpired later had Ted fired, and me sent to the penal colony a rig known as the Morecambe flame rotting away for the last 4 years way down in Holly Head harbour it happened after a good will gesture on our part as follows..

The remaining crews from the Piper were found temporary places on the Claymore, it was a hard time for the company but they did their best for the crews, However the ex-piper boys still worried for their jobs which Ted and I discussed with them on a number of occasions, finally it was decided Ted and I would be spokesmen we arranged a meeting in the cinema between the Rig superintendent and the crew. After the introduction by Ted he handed the floor over to me which took me by complete surprise, I could have wiped the smile off his face this was Teds sense of humour, it

was never mentioned as part of the proceedings was the first thing that went through my head looking over at Ted who now had an ear to ear smile on his face, he was having a laugh, so I explained why the crew were worried and handed the floor over to the crew for questions the plan being the super would pass the concerns to the office in town. So, we all thought, later that day Ted and I bumped into a service hand who asked us

"are you two the lads that arranged the meeting in the cinema?"

"we are" I told him proudly

"I was in the office at lunch while the super called town, the boss in town only seemed interested in who organized the meeting not the issue"

That left us somewhat puzzled

Ted, "I'm puzzled, Mike, I was not expecting that,"

I was well pissed off, "I think I'll go see Chris".

Ted laughed, "good idea Mike you can go home today,"

The next trip Ted never returned, the trip after that, I was transferred to Hollyhead I was told to report to the wreck called Morecambe flame a jack-up rig which had been left to rot in the harbour for 4 years.

This was my first experience on a Jack-up rig began with me arriving in Hollyhead by car at 20.00hrs it was dark pouring with rain my first impression of Holly head was not good, as I drove through the centre I witnessed several incidents from fighting to women screaming the odds through bedroom windows at drunken men in the street. I located the scruffy B&B, at the docks the room was very basic it reminded me of the local charity shop, all dissimilar furniture not even the bed clothes matched the pillows, I looked closer it was festooned with hair and stains likely from some drunk picking his nose, I had the landlady change the bedding clearly she was loving all the attention from these North sea tigers, she was dressed in the shortest and close fitting mini skirt, she dared wear like she was on a night out, her husband green with jealousy

"I will deal with this Vicky"

she ignored him loving all the complimentary remarks made at her from the riggers competing for her attention. The next morning, I made my way down to the dock side I arrived at the Jack up called the Morecambe Flame, along with 6 other guys everyone sheltering from the spray from the waves that crashed into the dock breakwater. Spray soared overhead battering the company van hard, rocking it violently it was in danger of getting washed into in the dock along with my car, so I quickly moved it to safer ground.

We were all soaked by the time Gordon the Chief unlocked the gang plank, I rushed up the gangway onto the rig to get away from the spray the first thought that came to me was "hell what a heap of crap" it was just rust everywhere I looked. The chief Mechanic introduced himself to us I already knew him and some of the others. The chief "Gordon" turned to me and Marty the welder. Gordon turned to me,

"First thing we need to do is open up the accommodation"

"Mike you and Marty" (Marty the welder) open the watertight doors".

The Other guys were sent to Sort out lighting powered from the dock and of course they all complained because they were all soaking wet, they should not be handling electrical cables,

"it's dangerous" a young electrician complained (in those days safety was still lip service only) no one paid any attention. Marty soon had the watertight door welds cut free, he looked up at me with a quizzical smile, and said:

"what the Fuck we going to find in here Mike"!

we opened the door to the accommodation we were overwhelmed by the most horrendous stink it had us all coughing our lungs up, our eyes were smarting.

"let's give it a couple days to air off," I said.

Gordon stood behind us smiling, breathing masks were thrust into our hands.

"Come on you wimps get in there find out if we can get this pile of crap running, I know you Mike I'm sure you'll sort it out."

It was quite nerve racking entering the accommodation, all dark and foreboding just like in the Alien film, the floor was slippery from the rat shit, the rats were scurrying away in all directions over our boots and out the door.

"how the hell did they get in?" Marty shrugged.

These rigs have steel covers that can be swung down over the port holes for protection, in high seas it was black as pitch inside, I am sure the crews had just dropped whatever they were doing and left the rig. The lockers were still locked boots and clothes strewn over the floor dirty plates on the dinner tables, no wonder the rats were at home here, everywhere it was stinking to high hell, we all felt like throwing up once we had all the doors and port holes open we left it to air for a few days.

There was another watertight door on the deck which we opened and descended down into the Machinery in the lower decks it was dark and also smelly, once through a couple more doors I came to the engine room. I stepped through the door into 2 inches of water. It was just like the Alien film where the engineer was searching for the cat in the dark, there was a constant echoing to the slightest sound the wind was whistling outside which made it even scarier. Marty and I went through to the high voltage switch room it was also in 2 inches of water it would be highly dangerous if the rig was operational, so the first job was to pump out the water then find out how it came in.

A week later the Rig Manager (Terry same guy from the Claymore) made a spot check on us at night and caught the night watchman fast asleep naturally he was fired. Terry did not suffer fools, he was a very strict by the book American, we all came to respect him strict he was, but he also looked out for us.

The plan to commission the rig ready for drilling in Morecambe Bay was now official we had a 4-year contract. Terry appointed me the night watchman so there I was with the short straw the entire crew thought it was hilarious as they saw my disappointment (I hated night shift). Sentenced to be on my own all night on this stinking smelly rig, there was an old porter cabin at the top of the gangplank. It was to be my office for the coming 12-hour shift, a radio and a very large Mobile phone for company it was for "Emergencies only" Terry told me firmly.

I knew complaining would make no difference, so I resigned myself to my fate, I had to do a walk around the rig every few hours that was my only task.

A few weeks later the rig was progressing well. I had just started my lonely shift in the dark it was windy the spray came crashing over the decks of the rig, I decided to do my inspection around the rig, I descended down the very steep stairs to the poorly lit lower decks, I froze I could hear a faint voice, there shouldn't be anyone here I thought unless there was a thief about! My imagination was working overtime as it does when you're tired, I sneaked carefully through the big heavy watertight doors hoping not to be heard by the violent robbers who were armed to the teeth waiting to crucify me.

"it's just your imagination" I kept telling myself,

at this point I have to say I was terrified it was dark the wind whistling outside a chain tapped the hull armed with only a pathetic little torch but determined to press on or should I call Terry!

"No, I will check it out," I convinced myself.

The voices were louder now I could hear chuckling the sweat was running down my face as I picked up a 2 metre length of pipe for a weapon, as I approached the door to the electricians office where the voice was coming from, I kicked the door open and yelling at the top of my voice,

"I have you now bastards".

I came face to face with a radio and nothing more, it had been left on, but all the same it had scared the shit out of me. I continued as watchman a few more weeks then we all moved on board the rig.

I stopped the night shift the accommodation still had the dreadful smell it lingered on even with all exits open, 24 hours a day a fortune was spent on air fresheners, we lived on microwave dinners yummy. We moved the rig to the centre of the harbour so the nights out on the town stopped.

One night the crew escaped to town, led by our new chief engineer who was desperate for booze they took one of the 52-man Lifeboats and moored it to the dock, eager for the party beckoning uptown. I had to remain onboard to look after the engines. At 5am it was getting light I decided to get some air and enjoy the morning sun on the main deck, as I stepped through the water tight door I came face to face with the image of Terry the manager for a moment we both frozen in surprise he had a piercing stare I broke the ice

"Morning Terry did you have a good drive",

that was me trying to be cool.

"yes, Mike I did are you alone? where the hell is the crew?"

I was desperately seeking a reply but my mind was a blank from shock so I said nothing he wondered around the deck so I followed him then it all became painfully clear as Terry stopped dead in his tracks, I could see his body go tense, I could or most see the steam streaming from the managers ears as he stared in rage at the startling distant image of the bright Orange lifeboat hanging by one end from the dock, the tide had gone out leaving the boat hanging like a Pendulum, the hull had been smashed by the swell of the ebbing tide. The crew just lined up along the dockside admiring their handy work. I had to make a quick exit to conceal my laughter it was lucky for me I had remained behind to watch the engines. Terry was beside himself with rage he called the whole crew into the galley once the bad boys had returned via the local Tugboat. I could read the dread on the faces of the crew clearly expecting the worst and that is what they got. The chief Engineer got fired the rest of the crew all received written warnings and fired.

That left just me and Gordon to run the rig. (Gordon was at home on leave).

Terry thanked me for being a

"kiss arse"

I was alone again until Gordon arrived a week later with some electricians and Mechanics; we had the rig ready in a month. It was during this time I met a great friend and Mechanic, Freak de Hann he towered over us all at 7foot 2".

We made it to location late by only 2 weeks, that's good for the North Sea, the rig drilled for 4 years at various locations in Morecambe Bay it was hard work for Mechanics old rigs always are.

I felt the return of the Grim Reaper stalking me on more incidents yet again it started at high tide 10 am this day, I had to launch a lifeboat accompanied by two roustabouts and tie up to a standby vessel, while the lifeboat davits were weight tested. Myself and the two roustabouts played cards and watched porn with the crew on the standby vessel, five hours later I got the call to return, but one doubt played on my mind as I looked across at the rig a mile away it suddenly dawned on me the rig seemed much higher, this would not be a simple operation firstly these life boats are not designed to go back plus the tide had gone out, the rig was easily 20 feet higher now and the 15 feet swell made it or most impossible so it would be difficult to reattach it to the Davit hooks

+ "we will need to stay here the roustabouts insisted we will never get hooked on in this"!

I radioed the Skipper

"come on over he insisted it will be ok it's not that bad" It never looks that bad when you're looking down from 80 ft above, The biggest worry was that the current could carry us under the rig, and onto the huge gear teeth on the legs of the jack up, I urged him. He was not convinced, like a fool I replied,

"it's much scarier from here skipper but I'll give it a try,"

, worse was, yet to come as I boarded the lifeboat my boots filled with water, there was a leak the floorboards were floating, I could see the inrush of water below the drive shaft, I knew it was the stern gland the water was freezing, as I reached down into the water to feel for the gland nut, fortunately, I managed to screw it back in place and stop the leak, it took us hours of hand pumping to clear it. The boat bobbed about like a cork the tide had turned so I decided it was worth a try, as I approached the rig, the wind and swell drove the boat towards the rig. which meant going under it, the fragile hull would crumple against the giant jacking gear teeth mounted on the rig legs. The retrieving hooks seemed a lot higher than when we left because the tide had gone out, it was a long shot but I decided the only way would be to bring the boat alongside the rig on top of a swell so that the two lads with me could grab the hooks and connect them, which would be very dangerous because as the weight snapped back onto the hooks the whiplash could break bones, I told the boys of my plan they weren't happy. I took a wide circle so the boat would be on parallel course with the rig as I approached compensating for the current which seemed determined to dash us against the huge rig legs looming rapidly toward us, I must admit I was scared stupid I had a vision of my gravestone epitaph reading

"Killed while doing something really stupid"

I could not let my fear show to the boys, I had to appear in control I swerved away losing my nerve at the last second, the hooks crashed against the fragile hull the lads scowling at me.

"Shit Mike" they screamed

"you will never do it you will kill us all Mike"

I slammed the lifeboat into full speed 5 knots, it took 4 further attempts to get the timing right, on the fifth attempt I did it the boat felt like it would snap in two from the shock load of the wave vanishing from beneath us. Once safely back onboard my hands still shaking, I shouted at the Barge Engineer,

"why didn't you check the tide and weather before we left" he laughed "you r such a wimp Mike" and walked off.

I had a call out one morning, it was 3 am, Mike number 2 the night motorman rushed into my cabin.

"Mike can you meet me at the 2nd level shower room now please,"

I was not prepared for this, the smell hit me first a scene that no one wants to see, the floor was an inch deep with piss and shit,

"Mike what the hell is going on,"

"the toilets are blocked,"

"really I would never have guessed,"

This shower room had 6 toilets and six sinks and shower cubicles, there was a small strip 1 inch high under the door and all this piss was about to breach it and make a break for it down the corridor! I looked at all the toilets each one was full the smell was overpowering

"It must be blocked in the main pipe below Mike, Get two radios I'll go and connect the air supply from below, you stay here and guide me, and I'll open the air valve hopefully it will clear it".

Once the airline was connected, I called Mike on the radio,

"Mike are you ready I will just crack the valve when you tell me"

"ok open it then," his voice was unsteady he was nervous who wouldn't be, in a scene where you are about to be covered with loads of other people's excrement.

Hiss, I could hear the air passing through the valve

"It's moving open it some more" Mike shouted over the radio

"yes, that's getting it,"

"I tell you what give it a full blast for a second or two"

"Here it comes Mike" I shouted visualising all the crap shooting from the toilets covering him and the ceiling.

All I heard then was a horrible scream over the radio, I closed the valve, I ran all the way up the six decks to the shower room, I threw open the door there he was just as I thought, covered with shit and piss running down his hat and face, the entire ceiling was peppered with small lumps of shit and toilet paper, I tried not to laugh, Mike took a step closer so I held out my arm to stop him,

"Keep your distance Mike I don t need this"

The toilets were clear at least, so I sent mike off to get cleaned up, while I called the night steward to come and clear up the mess, this should be funny when he sees this, I waited until he arrived walking up the corridor towards me with the usual belligerent steward attitude. I casually pointed to the shower room shaking my head, "you better get this cleaned up mate," he looked like he had just woken up as his hand pushed open the door, I could feel the laughter welling up inside me, watching his face and the look of sheer horror that adorned his entire being, revolted by the site that faced him he froze for an instance, then he turned to face me I could swear there was a tear in his eye.

"Mike the night motorman." I said and nodded.

"also, its 5 am so you better hurry the crews will be along shortly."

I could see the panic welling up in the steward's face.

"Fuck this" he shouted.

I walked off at that point I had to laugh as I shut my cabin door a floor up from the sewer on the top level.

Two trips later we were skidding the drilling derrick onto a platform with the hydraulic jacks, I was working with a big Mechanic from Scotland he was a very big lad all of 6' 6" 16 stone, We were trying to disconnect a coupling with two 36 inch pipe wrenches unaware the toe cap of my boot was trapped under a small gap in the decking which was 12 inches higher than the one my other foot was on, I heaved down on my wrench, it slipped off hurtling me backwards as I fell backwards my foot remained flat on the deck, I heard my ankle snap as my back hit the deck some 12 inches lower than my other foot, the pain shot through me like a bullet. I saw blood running down my boot, the Scottish Mechanic, Simon a giant of a man grabbed me, picked me up like I was nothing and carried me to the sick bay, by now the pain was that bad I had sweat pouring down my face, but as all North sea tigers, one does not scream out, just a grimace and swearing is allowed Simon just dumped me on the bench,

"there ye go pussy," he laughed.

The medic cut my boot off, the look on his face said it all.

"what a mess," he exclaimed,

"fuck Mike it's very a bad break I'm not sure what can be done,"

he lowered the large mirror, so I could see the bits of bone sticking out through the ripped flesh, it looked awful.

That was me off work for 6 months, and a further 3 months light duties. By the time I got back working normally the crew were preparing to move the Rig, we jacked the rig down onto the water using our buoyancy to pull the legs out of the seabed, but they were too deep in the mud, I was at the water tower on deck, the sea was only 6 inches from coming over the side. The Barge op stopped jacking, "wait" he said, "see if she comes up on her own."

 She did but only the port side, so my side the starboard dipped under the sea, a wave came rushing at me I attempted to run for safety but there was nowhere to go! looking up I could see the Derrick moving it moving across the sky to my great relief it stopped as the water came up to my thighs, damn it was cold, I managed to get to the highest point out of the water. It was 4 hours before the starboard side eased up out of the mud, allowing the rig to level out. As the legs slowly emerged above the deck, in the gusset work in the lower structure that had spent so much time submerged, very large crabs and lobsters had wedged themselves in the corners. It was funny watching the roughnecks struggling to prize them out, our Portuguese cook showed us how to get them out by pouring fresh water over them. Choppers had been circling the Jack up entire time. I suppose they were expecting to see the rig turn turtle, later that day lady luck arrived, and I got off only to be met by a large crowd at the Blackpool heliport, they were hoping for a story so I gave them one I tried in vain to make myself out to be the hero, but failed, it's strange how one's short of words when confronted by microphones. I just hope they understood Klingon (star trek) because I'm sure that's how it must have sounded or maybe I Just ran off at the mouth, I think it's' called verbal Diarrhoea. A few years later we took the rig to Greenock where it was to be decommissioned. The electrician and I were left to maintain the rig, hopefully to prevent rust covering the entire rig and machinery rendering it useless, it's called a dry watch routine it took two years. During that time, myself the electricians and one other mechanic rented a house in Greenock the idea was that two of us would remain with the rig for 2 weeks and get relieved by the other two. The house only lasted 5 months it was burgled 3 times on one occasion we were still in bed it's a rough area! Matt the Mechanic from Glasgow tried to convince us he could sell all the engine spares to the local Mafia,

"yes of course you can Matt," I laughed, to my great surprise just a few days later these really hard looking nut cases arrived at the Rig gangplank.

"Hey Jimmy" they yelled

I looked over to see these shady looking Glaswegians, boy did they look mean the bigger one had scars all over his face bald headed, a part of his left ear was missing, he had a large ring through the other ear, the second one had long black hair and a big moustache complemented by a set of gold teeth.

"See you boy, let us on board or ill kick your head in"

"what can you say"

"ok, right then come up" I said and opened the gate,

"where's Matt the wee bastard."

Matt turned up before they made it to the top of the gangplank

"leave this to me" Matt insisted.

so, he showed them down to the void spaces down below where the spares were. There was easily £10,000 worth of spares, Stuart and I stood back to watch the negotiations take place with the gangsters, It didn't seem to bother Matt that these guys all carried guns, you could see the bulge at the back of their shirts the gangsters looked over the spares,

"I 'll give you £3000 for the lot" scar face growled

"ok then" matt replied quickly,

The scar told Matt, "I 'll have someone pick it up tomorrow you will need to get it on the quayside for us,"

as he stared daggers at Matt.

From the rough end of Paisley himself, Matt tried to match the stare. Stuart who was stood next to me, nudged me and winked as if to say there's gonna be trouble, I decided to break the deadlock

"ok pal I 'll get it all stacked quayside by tomorrow,"

"I'm not your Pal Sassenach, call me when it's done."

ignoring the remark, I said, "there's a fenced off area in the hanger we will stack in there ok,"

the scar gave me a piercing stare,

"make sure you do, right"

He gave me a second glance, nodded to his men and the gangsters left. We managed to get the spares stored in the area inside the hanger as promised by the next day we all decided to go home for the weekend because we hadn't heard from the Gangsters.

Monday morning, I returned on my bike, as I passed through the gate the security guard pulled me over,

"Mike there's trouble there's been a break-in Management are all over the place so watch out,"

I rushed through to the hanger it was empty Matt stood at the fenced area in silence I went over "what are you going to tell scar face Matt"?

I had to laugh he was pale

"fuck off Mike it was that bastard Scarface, that took it and everything else so there'll not be a pay-off."

"How do you know that"

"Scare face called me, laughing his head off", then hung up."

During this job I had been commuting at the week ends on my motorcycle, a couple months later as I sped out of a village in the Scottish borders, I was enjoying the ride when bang! I found myself soaring through the air then an almighty thud as the bike crashed into the ground dragging me with it. I woke up at home in time to hear twisted metal hitting the ground outside the house, the farmer had kindly brought my bike or ex-bike, home perhaps by way of an apology.

"Ah! What about my fucking shoulder"?

the pain had just dawned on me

"give me drugs" I shouted,

the pain was so great later I did get drugs from my loving screaming skull of a wife just so I could get the train back to the rig in Greenock. That night the pain got to me again, so I crawled off to the A&E in Gourock.

"wait in here" the orderly told me,

two male night shift hospital nurses who were clearly Gay judging by their clothes, stood over me.

"Sorry pal but your arm needs pushing back in place and guess what it's going to fucking hurt like hell, so Bruno the hulk here will hold you down and I will pop the arm back in its rightful place,"

Boy did it hurt, in fact I fainted, but soon as I came around, I checked myself out just in case well you never know with these gay types? They had in fact left me a packet of painkillers.

"You ok Jimmy" Bruno laughed

"take care of that arm."

Every time I moved the arm I got a nasty pain shooting up the side of my neck just like an electric shock, causing me to jump, of course anyone seeing this thought I was some sort of nut case, The pain got that bad I left Stuart the rig sparky with the rig and I went home.

"I hope you're not losing pay now your home"

was all I got by the way of sympathy from my loving wife. Use the arm as much as possible until the tissue has worn away, My Doctor told me to go swimming.

So, I did, every day for a month, I got to know some local wives during the swimming, which turned out be a regular thing, and a laugh too, however, it was not to last. One wife Marion, with the big boobs asked me if I would give her lift on the bike to the baths next time, it was fine by me, those large breasts pressing into my back-mm mm. This day Lunch time arrives, I had forgotten about this arrangement. my wife the screaming skull had come home for lunch unannounced, to unload her stress on me, and our four boys, there's was a knock at the door, she answers it seeing the magnificent cleavage filling the doorway she asks,

"hello can I help,"

"Is Michael ready for the baths he's giving me a ride"

"I'll stop you right there."

The screaming skull interrupted the cleavage then turned to me and said at the top of her voice "Michael I think it's time you went back to work your shoulder must be fine by now."

 then slammed the door in the cleavages face.

Holland

I met the crew at Schiphol airport, we must have looked like a collection of North Sea rejects, we were greeted by the Canadian Tool pusher Byron Henderson, he was about my height, black hair and small moustache, he had a friendly face but looks can be deceiving, over the following four years he turned out to be a great boss.

"Hello suckers" he laughed and dropped into the nearest chair,

"I'm your boss for the Ensco70 Jack up, I assume you are all headed, there, the rigs in a real mess it's come up from Africa where there are no regulations, so it's not fit to work here in the Netherlands so it's gonna be a hard slog boys I been working Rigs my whole fifteen years so has my Pa (His Father), I never even seen the fucking rig so I'm pretty much in the dark like you fellas, we can assess it once we're there, but for now I'll get the beers in," He smiled then beckoned a waiter.

33

After a two hour taxi ride we arrived on the Ensco 70 Jack up berthed in Rotterdam, the OIM (offshore installation Manager), Irvine Stuart, another great boss from Canada, it turned out he and Byron knew each other, so after introductions Irvin gave us all the low down on the state of the rig. He toured us around the rig, the accommodation was smelly but it was normal rig smell a mixture of strong coffee and oil base mud, the youngest of our little group of ten, was John Lewis from a tiny fishing village north of Aberdeen, he was clearly still wet behind the ears he blurted out,

"I'm not fucking living here its filthy,"

laughing the Canadian was casual in his reply with a smile he laughed,

"well fuck off home then sonny,"

we all laughed.

Donny the most hardened rigger of us all clearly found all this very amusing, smiling at John he laughed,

"you will not be on my crew then laddie, Ya big soft Lune ye are,"

we were shown to our cabins I shared with anther Mechanic Alan from Preston; he was a typical lad from the school of hard knocks. A lad from Lancashire, and very outspoken, a great sense of humour he was a bit shorter than me, in fact much alike me in many ways he was a hardened biker too. We donned work gear and mustered on the deck as instructed in front of a yank called Snake, he sat on a drum smiled.

"My names Jim Morrison and no I'm not from the "Doors" group, so call me "Snake," glad you're all so keen on work, I've just received a deadline to get the rig ready for drilling, but there's no way it can be done in time, so we'll be late as normal, as it always is in the Drilling game, its near quitting time so let's have a beer, after that it will be heads down until we are done, ok lads."

The lot of us rushed off to Pekoes bar in Rosenberg, it is a small town just outside the yard, the bar was small but welcoming.

The cliental consisted mainly of women gays and prostitutes, the place was filled up to max, I'm sure most of them were locals. The next morning I felt awful God knows how Byron felt, he was in a drinking competition with this huge Dutch guy drinking beer laced with chilli powder, it certainly cleared him out internally, the septic tank was on max that morning, we all blamed him and the Dutch guy for the smell in the accommodation, also because he was the biggest of the crew, Freak the Dutch guy was over 7ft tall, he later became my assistant, he was a great lad, I still know him to this day, a good friend. The intention was to bring this rig up to spec so it could drill in Europe. It had recently returned from Africa where there are no regulations to control pollution or safety, It showed too what a wreck, the Jack up had a listing (The rig was tilted) water was discovered under the false floor(void space) on the bottom deck a hatch was removed a long length of rope was tossed at me Byron, chuckled.

"Mike you and Freak get down there and search for the leak, use the rope to find your way back."

Byron was about to rush off, I called him back,

"Maybe you haven't noticed but Freak is over 7 feet tall, the void has no more than 5' feet clearance, perhaps sends someone shorter"

Byron looked at me quizzically," You don't like Freak then,"

"yes, I do like him he's a good hand"

Freak laughed and gave me a frown,

"it's ok Mike I can do it,"

Byron gave me a side glance, "ok then, carry on Mike"

laughing he briskly walked off, which left Freak and I looking at each other in surprise and laughed, the Tool pusher had missed my very obvious point entirely, or did he do it deliberately for a laugh, I tied the rope off to a post, eased myself down into the cold water it came up to my waist.

I looked around into the dark foreboding void, I flashed the torch about I could see the 5-foot beams reinforcing the vessels structure, there were cut outs halfway up to crawl through to the next section it was the same in all directions.

"Shit we could get lost in here Freak, don't lose the rope Freak for Christ sake."

As we moved clear of the open hatch, we had to bend our heads to clear the roof in Freaks case his entire body, after climbing through the first access hole I was soaked right up to my chest, Freak really struggled to get through I kept looking for a disturbance in the water caused by the ingress of the sea, we passed through several access hatches before I heard the inrush of the water, it was then I realised the water was now up to my chest which scared me,

"we better hurry Mike before you drown,"

"why me?"

"I'm much taller, I might reach the access hatch before it reaches my head," Freak chuckled,

"very funny anyway you will still drown at the same time,"

I could see the leaking hatch cover ahead, I really hoped we could just tighten it to stop the leak, I was convinced we would never get back to the open hatch before we drowned. By the time we tightened it and stopped the leak the water had reached my chin the water was freezing my teeth were chattering, I looked up at Freak the giant, he looked down at me with a smile,

"see Mike, we are fine do you have the rope"

Panic swept over me as freak answered,

"no, I don't,"

Freak laughed,

"I have it, bet you shit yourself then eh Mike,"

"I hate you Freak; you just scared the shit out of me,"

we laughed, who was I kidding he could have folded me up and stuffed me in his pocket.

By the time we reached the access hatch my hands were numb the crew dragged me out of the water,

"Mike your lips have turned blue, best go to your cabin get a hot shower both of you."

Byron laughed; he ordered the crew to lower another pump down the hatch.

I spent the following 4 years on the 70 which taught me a great deal about jack up rigs, some of it, life threatening. Two years on we had a new Mechanic, a German guy who was somewhat older than the rest of us. He was called Horst Jaeger he certainly knew his stuff he later became famous for attending a rig abandonment exercise in the wrong clothes, (These exercises were carried out without warning every 2 weeks) on one drill Horst turned up in his pyjamas and dressing gown and furry slippers(it is mandatory to wear warm clothing) he stood there wondering what the Joke was all about. He, like most Germans had no sense of humour. The Electricians who worked hand in hand with myself and Freak, Tony the day electrician from Ireland (ex-Rugby player) he was a great laugh, also Kenny a real-life hooligan he got himself paralytic every crew change. I got into the habit of dumping him onto a baggage trolley, and race through Schiphol airport to leave him at his gate, of course, he was refused entry to the flight so I'd lay him down on a couch, call his wife and tell her he would be late home. It became routine every trip. My relief was Alan a great Mechanic a cool fellow he was about my age he lived not far from me before he moved to Spain, we had become a great team.

Courses are mandatory offshore, it had been decided by the powers that be that all Electricians and Mechanics would be the Lifeboat coxswains, (a week's course) in the Euro port, the four of us Including Horst marched down the jetty towards the life boats the instructor told us who ever is the Coxswain gives the orders and must be obeyed, "Horst" had a very strong German accent and of course soon as he shouted command's to us such as,

"I am giving the orders"

in the loud German accent, we all fell about laughing he was so pissed off he crashed the boat into a nearby barge which turned out to be occupied, the occupants were clearly not amused in the least, shouting and cursing Horst for his incompetence,

Red with rage, Horst jumped down from the wheelhouse, I assume to get to us, but the deck was wet from the collision he slipped over the side into the freezing water. Germans are by nature very proud people Horst included. we dragged him back on board, back in the locker room the instructor handed him a towel which he threw back at him, he stomped off in a rage swearing in German we just laughed even more.

He became a bit of a legend on board the 70 he could not get the steam generator to work, whereby Freak and I had taken time to master it.

The temperature had dropped a lot it was well below freezing in the docks. The Steam generator was our only source of heating, it enraged Horst that he struggled with it, he had to be the best after all he was German, he lived in dread during his shift should he be required to start it.

"Can't you manage without it"

he would tell the crew even though it was minus 10 degrees and the entire crew were freezing.

This day I was in a hanger 500 yards down the dockyard working on a crane. Freak burst in driving the forklift laughing himself silly, finally he managed to blurt out.

"Mike you better come back to the rig, Horst has scolded two welders by pulling the bypass on the steam generator,"

He continued laughing.

"Oh yes he has punched the sparky too, for suggesting he should ask you to show him how to run it, I'm not doing it its better watching him get angry,"

I jumped on board the forklift truck, we sped off to the rig reaching the stairs that lead down to the evil Steam Generator machine, I could hear Horst frantically trying to justify his scolding of the two French welders to the Tool pusher Byron who was dying to hear Horsts excuse. While the electrician listened nursing his split lip which Horst had inflicted while the electrician was holding back the two welders who were clearly after Horst's blood. I was trying hard not to burst out laughing when Horst saw me, he lunged for me saying,

"Mike you Englander swine you have been keeping secrets from me,"
it was that accent I could hold it back no longer, I laughed out loud
"Horst the war is over."

By this time Freak was in tears of laughter too, it spread to the tool pusher he too burst out laughing, the humiliation was too much for Horst, he marched off mad as hell, slamming the door behind him, closely followed by the two French welders we saw him later that day nursing a black eye.

The Rigs overhaul was complete, the next day was the open day so the local population could tour the rig, guided by our Senior Tool pusher John Riley. He was proud of his crews and the work that had been accomplished. The maintenance office (my office) was halfway down a flight of stairs leading on to the engine room. Horst was busy having a go at me for humiliating him in front of the Tool pusher the previous day, he lunged at me with both arms, I body swerved and got him in a headlock just as the door swung open, there stood the Tool pusher and some of the tourists looking on in shock, as they saw me holding Horst in a head lock, Tony the sparky, jokingly shouting,

"go on Mike get the German bastard."

I swear I saw the pushers jaw hit the floor; he quickly slammed the door shut. We all burst out laughing and forgot the issue at hand we were later that day given a verbal warning, from his lordship the Rig super he was a great bloke, John Riley, he worked by the book but had a sympathetic attitude. Later that week Horst was running around the deck trying to keep up with the backlog of routine work, (as a Mechanic on a jack-up rig, it can be a very stressful job), Horst was wearing his white hard hat and not the obligatory grey one.

"Horst,"
John shouted, "why are you wearing a white hat?"
Looking somewhat irritated,

Horst turned to face John and snapped,

"white hat! Fucking white hat, I've always had one"

Clearly to Horst it was a very trivial issue,

"anyway, what's the problem John, I'm busy,"

John told him "a grey hat is to be worn on board this rig,"

"Well if that's all you got to worry about John then you are ok, now fuck off I v got more important things to do than worry about a fucking hard hat so fuck off John."

Horst sped off across the deck, leaving John taken aback, John had never been spoken to like that before he stood speechless for a minute, looked down at the deck shook his head and went back to his office, unnoticed, from the deck above I had witnessed the exchange. I told Freak that evening,

"he will get fired soon Mike, I'm sure, John is also a very proud man he will not stand for that,"

Sure, enough Horst never returned after that trip.

The following new year's eve we were fogged in on the rig though the fog did clear a bit, so we boarded a boat for the docks, a 3-hour trip which left us the crew stuck on the dockside in Dan-Helder, (Holland). The rig manager turned up and gave us all some cash, (£300 each) "you are all booked in the Ibis hotel in Amsterdam there's no flights tonight so you will all be there on New Year's Day too. It turned out to be a great New Year's Eve. Walking around the red-light zone that night with Donny from Fort William and young John Munro a roustabout

Donny whispered in my ear, he paused then continued,

"he's got a very bad foot odour problem that young boy."

"yes, it's really bad I have shared a cabin with him, I v stopped him taking off his shoes in the Room,"

"can't be that bad" I laughingly replied,

"Oh yes, it is" Donny chuckled,

"Why are you telling me this important information Donny,"

"It's Johns Plan to go with a prostitute tonight, he's never done it before" he laughed (Donny had a very strong Scottish accent),

"you will see soon enough Mike."

It was raining we were stood in a very busy pub across the cobbled stoned alley from several windows where beautiful naked young women are on show, it was very noisy, so our voices were high,

"that one there" John shouts over the Pub noise,

"ok then off you go John, we will wait here for you,"
Donny killing himself laughing, he leaned over to me,
"watch this Mike, just wait he'll take off the trainers and John will be thrown out of there in a flash."
I could see John at the door talking a deal with the girl, then in he went shutting the door, at this point Donny is killing himself laughing
"it can't be that bad," I said to Donny,
"yes, it can keep watching,"
Sure, enough, the door opens, the girl rushed out into the pouring rain waring just underwear, clutching John's trainers she tossed them down the street, then quickly ushered John out the door. I just fell about laughing.
"aye happens all the time." Donny smiled.
A year later there I was, sat at my desk writing the daily log, the fire alarm went off, followed by an announcement that the fire was in the engine room. The Engine room is situated just yards from my desk, down several stairs, my first thought,
"fuck what do I do I should know this,"
I ran down the stairs to the door I opened the fireproof door a little, I could see fifteen-foot flames leaping up from number 2 engine, I followed the flames upward they were licking the overhead fuel tank! I could not get into the room far enough to shut the system down,
"shit shit,"
was all that came out of my mouth, I looked to the electrician his face was as white as a sheet, he threw his arms out,
"don't ask me!"
On the verge of panic, I phoned the fat controller (tool pusher) told him to hit the shutdown switch on the Drill floor
"No way" was the answer,
He was such a coward.
But then he was drilling, if the drilling just stopped the drill string would be stuck in the hole and it would cost millions to correct it. I ran back down to the engine room door followed by Jerry the stand in electrician, he was still pale, so I found myself face to face with the controls for Halon Gas bottles, (these are intended for this type of emergency and a last resort) I felt someone join me it was Freak and Alan the other mechanics,
"you need any help Mike we can't sleep with the alarm going off what the fuck have you done,"

"ha ha very funny," I exclaimed.

Freak took my arm,

"Mike use the Halon, you're in charge here do it now before the fuel tank blows up and kills us all."

I ripped open the doors there were four handles, so Freak took two I took the other two, we pulled with all our might on the release levers a loud bang rocked the room as 16,000 pounds of pressure shot from the cylinders, shaking me through my body right down to my toes, as the high-pressure gas was released into the engine room, at this point we all put our hands over our ears the scream of the rushing gas made a hell of a noise, my hands were shaking uncontrollably and the sweat pouring down my face. The fire was out the room was a real mess it was recommended not to enter the room for 12 hours this gas would kill a man if you were in the room with it. This gas has since been outlawed and of course it is very expensive. We all went back to the office the fat controller burst into my office, after the event shouting at me,

"do you know how much that Halon costs,"

"Yes, I do it's a lot less than a new rig" I shouted back,

"Lucky for you I was here to release it I am sure the company man will be pleased to hear how you refused to shut the rig down."

As it happened the company man had walked in the office just at that very moment.

"what was that you just said Kevin," he demanded

he held up his hand, "Kevin (the fat controller) you come with me now Mike, good work,"

off they scurried Kevin running along behind like a frightened puppy.

Boy it was so funny we all cheered he looked back cursing me

"I hope he gets the sack," Freak laughed."

I later found a cracked fuel pipe on number 2-caterpillar engine which caused the fire, so we replaced all the fuel pipes on all five of the engines.

A year later there was a downturn in the oil Industry, so the company tightened its belt and people were paid off and of course the fat controller made sure I was one of them! But I did get my little bit of revenge, I found several crabs in the engine sea water strainers, so I placed all five of them in his bed before I left. 6 months at home while my four young boys ran riot, while their mother went off to work in a new restaurant in Berwick upon tweed. I spent most of my time restoring old Motorcycles and swimming. I also started cooking not my favourite job, but we had to eat, their mother was working all hours. So I was a house husband, it was great don't let women tell you how hard it is staying at home doing housework and chasing naughty kids it's great fun, I had it all organised, I overhauled one bedroom a day in turn plus the rest of the house (it was an old converted 17th century Millinery shop five bedroom) , washing done by lunch time. off I went to the local baths for a swim. It came to an end one night while eating our spag bog the boys agreed my spag bog was better than their mums, there was a sudden silence at the dinner table. The boys realised a line had been crossed, their mothers face was slowly turning red with rage, is this the woman I married, or a demon possessed? She thought she was the best chef in Scotland, so you can imagine the damage done to her massive ego, the tension broke when Sam, my eldest son started laughing, she leapt up from her seat like a raging bull,

"get to bed"

she yelled at the boys who by now were all laughing uncontrollably, they ran off.

"I hope you're happy now you have poisoned their minds against me you must go offshore again you have been too soft with the boys they hang on every word you say, Motor crossing, swimming in the river, playing hide and seek in the pitch dark, they are like wild animals."

I could see where this could end up so off, I went. I searched furiously for work offshore for what seemed like an eternity.

My eldest son Sam had joined the Army he was not happy with the treatment he got, so he told his brothers not to join the Scots Dragoon Guards, when the twins went to the careers office in Preston a year later, they made it clear they would not go to the Scots DGs and why, it somehow got back to Sam's Commanding officer, who was not impressed. Sam was ordered to the captain's office, the Captain demanded he call the twins and tell his brothers how great it was, if he refused his life would be made a misery. But Sam being Sam did call them but instead of carrying out his orders he told them the situation before the Captain could stop him, he shouted "it's crap don t come,"

So, his life was made a misery by one certain NCO and his Mole. My boys are close, so the twins joined up just to save Sam from the toffee-nosed morons they call officers that make up our armed forces. There were further incidents once the boys were reunited at the camp. Sam got his revenge, while on man-overs Ben made an error while driving a tank the NCO wrenched Ben from the cab and threw him to the ground, (Ben was a skinny little lad) Matt his twin ran to fetch Sam all 6 feet 2 of him, he threw the NCO aside, took Ben and all the witnesses to the Camp Commander to explain, later the NCO was transferred. The NCO's mole got a beating from Sam in the parade ground while the twins prevented the other NCOs from interfering. Soon as I heard of this, I called the officer concerned and in no uncertain terms I made sure he knew how I felt and my disappointment at such infantile behaviour from an Army officer. I had been brought up by strict officer I know how the system works so I may take things further should there be any more incidents. Yes, my boys had inherited my wild side my dear wife told me so.

"No wonder there's always some trouble where ever they seem to go even now, you are still the same Michael you are always involved in some sort of incident, you'll be killed one day you need to calm down you're like a big kid,"

she shouted

"So, you want me to stay at home then?"

"God no it's too late now the damage is done"

she stormed off.

Brazil

Eventually, a position turned up on a drill ship offshore Brazil, I'd never had the pleasure of a drill ship, so I decided to take a chance and go for it. I was so pleased with myself that night I tipped toed up to the bedroom threw off my clothes and slid into bed with a wide grin on my face,

"why have you got that stupid grin Michael,"

So, I told her the great news,

"you selfish sod you mean you will be jetting off to other countries while I am here on my own for a month at a time, what if something happens to you, how will we manage our bills, anyway I could not

cope with the boys alone when they are home, their much bigger now and they argue with me, Michael they gang up on me!"
 The other day they locked me in the Bathroom for 4 hours."
I had to laugh at that she started to cry at this point, so I cuddled her she shrugged me off.
"oh no, I know you! You just want sex, so forget it".
"Think of the money love, you could buy an exercise bike,"
I said jokingly thinking it would lighten the mood,
"So, I'm fat now is that it, you want this job so you can meet up with foreign women who are not fat or had 4 kids."
I burst out laughing at this,
"where did you get that from maybe I should have you sectioned then committed to an asylum."
so much for lightening the mood, of course, arguing with Dawn was a daunting prospect she was a demon, stubborn and very quick witted I rarely got the better of her.
The boys were on leave and were running riot around the house, I sneaked out to the stable situated behind our 17th century house, I had converted the stable into a workshop where I restored old motorcycles in-between repairing the boys motor crossers, but I rarely made it to my little escape
"Michael the phone"
It was work I got my instructions for Brazil; After the 6-hour flight I met a few other guys on their way to the same ship, outside the Rio Airport. A big fancy coach met us great I thought it's a double Decker I 'll sit at the front so I'll get a good view, a tap on my shoulder it was Don the electronics expert we hadn't been introduced,
"no don't sit their Mike you might get shot"
 "What you mean!"
"in the jungle the bandits take shots at the driver, if they get him, we get robbed but it's rare they manage it, my names Don by the way I'm the sparks."
looking closer I could see the bullet impacts on the glass, I thought here we go another bad call, maybe I should have stayed on the dole, too late now, better carry on,
Eventually, we arrived at the oil capital of Brazil 4 hours later in Macae,

Frazier the Ships Skipper told me, "a warning Mike, don't piss the locals off, it's only a fiver to have someone bumped off here, and drive by shootings are a common occurrence."

Once disembarked at the chopper base the place was crawling with people from so many Countries and Ethnic groups it was hard to tell who the goodies were, all hanging around the wide entrance to the Heliport the cool breeze blew straight through it.

Women dressed to attract attention, hoping to catch an oil man, and many did, the women are very sexy, there were young lads hoping for a job even if it meant having someone bumped off so they could replace them on the crew. Goings on outside the main entrance really shocked me, there were young boys in their early teens selling themselves to anyone for sex, men or women it was sickening. The crime in Brazil, it seemed was on a par with Nigeria. The river that passes through the town was black with pollution, the stink was so strong it took your breath away, to my horror further away downstream I could see children playing in it, looking back up the river I could see that the toilets from the houses dumped directly into the river not 200 yards from the children.

These same children sold drugs to survive, transactions took place quite openly and frequently outside the heliport. I was approached on several occasions I just ignored them of course. Don warned me about these children, they were used as part of assassinations, Some adult would pay them a few dollars hand them a Pistol, point out the target then walk off, leaving the child to carry out the shooting then throw the weapon in the river. In Brazil children under 15 could not be prosecuted.

Once we had boarded the very old chopper the two Brazilian Pilots walking towards us both tried climbing into the pilots seat, then started arguing who's turn it is to be pilot, a bleeding nose decided the outcome, it was like watching a keystone cops movie, I was killing myself laughing, but not for long there were no doors on these old choppers. Don nudged me and told me the history of these old choppers.

"These things regularly fall out the sky Mike, it has been known for these buggers to run out of fuel before they reach the base, because they got their sums wrong,"

Don Seemed cool with it so I thought why to worry now, I m a good swimmer least the waters are warm here, besides I was getting used to the Grim Reaper looking over my shoulder. We did arrive at the ship an hour later without any more arguments from the two pilots.

It was fucking hot all day long the sweat poured down my face, fortunately I had a helper Billson, from the Cameroon he was very black, you could barely make him out at night, just his shiny white teeth, he called me as I walked across the Helideck.

"White man Mike Mechanic over here,"

He greeted me with a huge friendly smile vigorously he shook my hand,

"You are Mike the danger man, I hear all about your trouble from the English folk here, I am Billson your assistant,"

"Thank you, Billson, it's nice of you to meet me do you know my cabin location?"

"of course, Mr Mike I will take your bag come please,"

After a week I was getting used to the workings of a drill ship and the rest of the crew, some Dutch some Scots and a few yanks, the Skipper Frazier, from Brecon, he was mad as a March hare. The accommodation was run by Brazilian women, they were very sexy they loved to dance, any music they heard they immediately started gyrating from their hips, it worked very well several of them married expats.

It was getting hotter as the trip progressed, I could not bear it, so I climbed down one of the escape ladders into the clear blue sea it was so wonderful

"ah!"

Billson cried out.

"Mr Mike, Mr Mike, please come back you will be eaten very soon sharks live here."

Shear horror propelled me up the ladder, turning around I saw a large fin cruising not twenty feet away, least I was cool now, standing in a pool of water I felt a tap on my shoulder, the skipper turned up looking a bit perturbed.

"Mike these ladders are for Emergencies, so if you're too hot let me know and I will lower a cage over the side for you,

Next day we had a supply boat arrive, delivering casing, (Casing is Pipe used to line the drilled hole,) for the hole we were drilling. Rumour had it that booze could be obtained on board, but I found it hard to believe, everywhere else I had been it was banned. Some months later I was coming down the stair from the bridge, the crane was bringing a load of pipe on board and I could see through the end of the pipe, as it swung across the deck of the ship, I could see cases of booze inside the pipe it was so close I could read the label on the crates, what made it funny was that Tool pusher was stood at the side of the deck as all this illegal booze passed not 2 meters above his head. Later that evening after I had finished my shift, I went to see the deck foreman a Danish lad called Life.

"Hey life mate, where's all the booze then?"

"It'll be 2 dollars for a bottle of Bacardi, hang on Mike, how do you know about that?"

"I saw it in that last load of pipe today, you do know it's illegal on-board don t you,"

"ok I 'll give you one bottle a week,"

"fine and a bottle of coke of course."

So, from then on, every evening my entertainment was a Bacardi and coke while listening to a letter from America on BBC radio, it was a crap reception, but that was all I could get, even with the aerial wire dipped in the sea. The following 6 months past quite peacefully all be it busy with repairs it was a very old ship, I needed to speak to the driller, Hans, a , fella, he was about as laid back as you could get, he was late for the shift handover every day, his lunch took hours and he was frequently so drunk he could not find his way across the deck let alone the stairway to the drill floor. One day I found him laid out across the deck, he was out cold, the Brazilian crew had thrown a tarpaulin over him so he could not be seen. The Derrick hand was running the drill floor while the pusher was throwing a wobbler screaming,

"where is Hans Mike have you seen the German bastard anywhere?"

"err no I've not spoken to him all day"

which was true.

"The company man will be here soon, and I'll need answers for him on our progress,

I suggested he get the Geolgraph sheet,

(The graph sheet is a pen recorder on a clockwork drum that records the penetration rate and drilling speed and tonne miles of the drill string). Meanwhile, the deck crew had dragged the drunken German up to the roof of the bridge and sat him in a deck chair. When I finished for the day the Pusher angrily asked me to "find the fucking driller."

So I nipped up to see if the driller was still on the Bridge roof! he was still there but quite dead, his skin was horribly cold, and no pulse, the medic checked him over and decided it was a drug overdose, cocaine was easily obtained on board the Brazilian drill ships. The Police from Macae arrived the next morning for the investigation, they seemed nonchalant about it all as if it was a regular thing here, which it was apparently, they took his body away with them. The drilling company was dragged up to the oil companies office to explain this tragedy, which of course they had none, so some of the rig crews were replaced it was easy to do that back then but the new hands required training the effect of that was loads of injuries. A few months later everything seemed to be calming down after the Drillers death. It was an exceptionally hot day the new hand working the derrick was exhausted, so I thought I'd give him a break, climbing up the very high derrick ladder which I had done many times, but on this day in the Control room Frazier the skipper was having a fight with his pal the radio operator, one of them fell against the DP switch, which caused the ship to swing about throwing me off the derrick ladder 60 ft. down to the sea! I did grasp the safety cage, but the force wrenched my wrist, so I let go and I plunged backward into the blue sea yelling my head off to attract attention. My impact on the sea nearly knocked the breath out of me I quickly rose to the surface I looked around to find the ship I could see it moving away in fact it was me who was moving, the water was actually quite warm, at first I thought this is ok but where's those fucking sharks, plus the current was so fast I could see the ship falling behind me at a rapid rate of knots. This scared the hell out of me what was worse still was the huge body of a whale speeding past me along with several of its family, forgetting that whales are harmless for a moment I nearly shit myself. One does re-evaluate one's priorities during an experience like that, I was startled as I was pulled out of the sea into the fast rescue boat by the Skipper and coxswain, I had been so transfixed by the whale I hadn't notice the approach of the fast rescue boat. I was in shock for a good few hours after, the jaws of a shark were never far from my legs each time I relived that moment in the south Atlantic. A year later the ship had relocated further south we had been warned of possible Pirates, it was middle of the night, I was woken suddenly by a loud bang and ripping sound echoing through the hull of the ship lots of shouting and slamming of doors I was sure there was gunfire.

I was so scared and confused I had no idea what I should do or where to go,

"find people"

was my only thought, running out of the cabin I ran straight into Frazier we tumbled to the floor?

"get off Mike,"

he looked as confused as I was,

"what the fucks going on Frazier,"

"I thought I was about to be captured by these pirate bastards I nearly shit myself Mike you idiot,"

"Pirates are you fucking kidding,"

"No, I am not come on we need to see if they v boarded us."

"Fuck off it's not the Spanish armada you know there are no pirates these days it's just myth."

"Ya think Mike look out there,"

looking over the side all I could see was the back end of a ship disappearing into the darkness.

"That's not a pirate,"

I laughed

"it could be any stupid sod falling asleep on the bridge."

It turned out in the end, that we had been rammed by another ship which ripped a large hole in our hull on the water line, but there are Pirates around the south Atlantic, so I'm told. We had all panicked at first, but it turned out no one had boarded the ship the other vessel had speed off into the night.

"They are welcome to it fucking piece of rusting shit anyway let the bastard sink,"

laughed Frazier

The hole was big enough to walk through and the water level in the switch room was raising fast,

"There's only one Bilge pump working, I found out why, stupid sods fitted the new pump wrong way up the motor should be above the pump and it burnt out."

I told Frazier he just laughed.

"We will need to ballast her over to keep the hole out of the sea,"

So, for the next 2 days we all walked about at 11 Degrees. The ship docked in the smallest shipyard I've seen, Aerio De carbo in southern Brazil the town was very small. It looked the type of place the

Brazilians came on holiday beautiful golden beach with about twenty bars along the promenade. I asked the skipper if I could go have a look "ok but take Fritz the roughneck with you."

Fritz was a Brazilian with a German father hence the name, big strong lad he was, it was a bit concerning when I noticed the man bag dangling from his shoulder, not a good idea to make any assumptions, this chap would tear your head off, I am sure, he was a mean looking sod too. We sat at the first bar we came to also there was a good view of the bikini clad women on the beach, Fritz ordered a few beers boy where they welcome ice cool beer it was easily over 40 degrees in the sun.

"Ok Fritz what's with the bag mate,"

I very politely asked laughing,

he frowned at me "I will show you"

he said pulling out a very shiny Magnum 45 pistol,

"we need this," he smiled,

there's drive by shootings out here every day, they often pick on westerners like you Mike, but we ok with this big gun,"

"Have you ever used it" I quizzed him,

"oh yes a few times,"

"How many people have you shot!"

to my astonishment,

"Five" he said calmly,

"but only two of them died,"

he looked disappointed I must have looked shocked with my mouth agape; After a few more beers I decided to change the subject, I commented that the beautiful blue sea was hard to resist, so I dived in the warm water, I could see thousands of tiny fish part as I slid through the water, it was brilliant, if the folks back home could see this wow, it was like a movie small picturesque seaside town blue sea lovely Brazilian women in bikinis, golden sand, just like a dream. I wonder how long it will take the yard to repair the ship was my next thought, I could stay here until it's finished, hmm what a brill idea. I'll ask skipper later, I was brought back to reality by gunfire in the town, I saw Fritz running up the beach shouting "Mr Mike you must swim back to the boat there is trouble here."

It's a fair old distance across this bay, but I will need to risk it rather than face some crazy Brazilian with a gun. I was halfway across the bay, when I remembered the other danger that was even worse, these waters were home to sharks, this thought really terrified me I could swear there was something following me, Oh how one's imagination runs away with itself when you're scared.

I was so exhausted as I reached the ship, I could barely climb the 20foot ladder to the deck. Once on deck, Fritz, Frazier and Mike the spark was there to meet me, all of them in stitches of laughter.

"I see you're a fast swimmer Mike, you mug, that shooting was Fritz we had a bet on to see how good swimmer you are." Frazier chuckled.

"oh yes, the boss wants you down in the machine room he's not happy,"

"Mike you need to see the gap between the new panel and the hole in the hull it's over an inch wide,"

"ok just gimme a minute please."

They were right the gap was huge, So I told them,

"you'll not stitch weld that gap,"

I shouted take that fucking panel away,"

"Mike"! Fritz took me to one side he whispered,

"don't shout at these guys Mike, they 'll get pissed off and either cut your throat or shoot you, they're crazy you know."

I watched them for a minute.

"Right I see your point, well what if I explain to them that a 4 mm welding rod will not bridge a 25mm gap, do you think they will take me seriously," I laughed,

Fritz frowned,

"Mike you may not have noticed but these guys all have small backpack which they never remove, it contains their gun, machete plus a small amount of cocaine and least of all their lunch."

I found all this to be farfetched or he was winding me up for a laugh.

"Fritz, maybe you explain it to them I'll see you later in the sick bay" I laughed and made a quick exit.

Before the repairs were complete, I received instructions, which had me transferred to another ship. I was to go by taxi with an armed bodyguard. It is a very dangerous area, it was 4-hour drive to Macae. An hour on we came to a small village, we had to stop; I was never sure why, I asked my bodyguard.

"There's been an accident Mike it will take a few moments to clear" Hosie, the bodyguard looked worried.

51

Right outside my window I could see a women sat by the side of the road with 4 babies in a wooden wheelbarrow, all crying, I could see the swollen bellies, I felt very guilty, there I was in my taxi a world away from starving. The woman wearing rags no shoes she was in tears nobody walking by her seemed the least bit bothered, they just walked on by. Angry I leapt out of the car walked over to what looked like a shop, I bought 4 cartons of UHT milk and handed them to her, she was so happy she kept kissing my hand, I got back in the car.
 Hosie was not happy.

"Mike this place is not safe for you please stay in the car," we drove on, I watched as the people who were passing, her ripped the milk from her, I was outraged but what could I do? Life can be so cruel even to the innocent 4 babies!

"Still think there's a God."

I asked myself for the second time in not so many months.

It was my first trip on the Malenkova it was supposed to be a better ship but a lot more work, I was working alone, but a more laid-back atmosphere,

"Mike Mechanic call the rig floor"

came over the pa system every hour, such was the workload, I dialled the rig floor. The driller Nail, answered.

"Mike the auto derrick seems to be awful slow can you have a look."

he was always polite, but you knew he meant to do it now, Nail was from Newcastle hell of a nice bloke a biker like me, so we had many lengthy chats about our machines as all bikers do. As I ascended the derrick ladder carefully this time remembering what happened last time, I approached the steel door of the operators hut, the operator sat inside this small hut and controlled the hydraulic arms which moved the drill pipe into the elevators at the centre of the derrick, all was quiet I could see the top of the Brazilians head through a small window in the door, he was there ok so, maybe he's smashed, or just asleep, so I kicked the door open, it was not either of those things, he was jerking himself off, he looked so shocked and embarrassed as he spun round to see me laughing my head off, I leaned forward sneakily to pressed the loud speaker button, I announced loudly over the P A system.

"Nail I found the problem Mendes is jerking off so we can all rest easy now," everyone on the rig would have heard, Mendes never lived it down, I just wished I'd had a camera to see his face the moment the door opened, and he realised he'd been caught.

On one occasion the drilling had shut down for Political reasons we heard it was because the company man had no TV signal, however the eight expats, me included found ourselves at the heliport in Macae, it was completely deserted not a soul in sight on the street, so Don, the electronics expert called the office they sent us two taxis. So, a race to Rio with the four Dutch guys in one car and us four Brits in the other, the Dutch guys got the Mercedes and floored it while Frazier and Mike the other sparky, Don, and myself. Frazier insisted we stop for some beer so we fell a good 10 minutes behind the Dutch lads, the road snaked through the thick jungle we had to avoid the hundreds of potholes, which made the driving really dangerous so passing the odd truck was fraught with danger, but the biggest danger, our driver informed us was the many bandits waiting for an opportunity to rob a crashed car, or even if the car is too slow, they shoot the driver. It seems highway robbery still goes on in Brazil. Now I knew why they all drive like maniacs, thirty minutes later we saw the Mercedes parked at the side of the road, all the occupants watching the driver frantically changing the rear wheel,

"stop we will help" I asked the driver,

Frazier told our driver not to stop, he explained the danger of the bandits once again, we all agreed to carry on. It was evening when we arrived in Rio, we had 4 hours to kill before the flight so Frazier having been a merchant seaman for many years told us he knew some great bars around the harbour area, so it was agreed we would go have a look, we passed through some real rough areas, terrorist graffiti covered most of the buildings, Don and I were not too keen to leave the car. Frazier pointed out the bar he used to frequent so we approached the bar, It was on a corner open on 2 sides save a pillar in the middle, there was a waist high wall of full bin liners all along the pavement outside the bar it was stinking, it was a high step on to the pavement and a second one into the bar, this was so you could not quite see into the bar from the road apparently it made it harder to pick out a target from a car. The bar was busy with prostitutes waring miniskirts and high heels low cut tops showing off a healthy cleavage, it was very tempting but not tempting enough for me and Don. As soon as we sat down the women moved closer desperately trying to engage us in conversation, I found several notes in my pocket with phone numbers, but all in all it was fun. Paco the taxi driver spoke to the owner who brought beer and glasses to our table.

Don the sparky turned to Frazier and shook him free from the woman he was kissing,

Don grabbed Frazier's arm,

"Are you kidding Frazier, this place is filthy, look at the glasses man, I'm not using these, they stick to the table"

My fingers stuck to the bottle as I picked it up so Don had Frazier wash them, by this time the women were sitting at our table clearly they were desperate for business, but there was a problem they were real rough, not a good looker amongst them, one of the rougher women shoved her hand down Mikes trousers, that was enough he leapt up and demanded, we all leave right away for the airport, Don and I agreed, Frazier was nowhere to be seen.

"Where the fuck is, he," Mike growled,

I wondered around the bar and there he was, at the rear of the bar getting a blow job,

"we r leaving mate"

I told him,

"you better hurry Mike is really pissed off"

"Ok" Frazer was not happy having his blow job cut short.

He pulled up his pants, the woman started shouting at him for money,

"fuck off Woman," Frazier shouted back,

then there was a loud bang! She had a pistol pointed at him, I watched very nervously,

"I think you better pay up Frazier"

she walked up to him and relieved him of his wallet. Lucky for him she could have relieved him of his passport. As we sped off, he laughed.

"There's no money in it anyway my cash is in my pocket"

Don smiled knowingly at him

"where's your credit cards then Frazier,"

his face immediately changed to one of dread. I was not sure whether to laugh or feel sorry for him. Mike just laughed.

"you stupid sod Frazier."

The next trip I met Yan he was the Technical leader on board he was from ST Petersburg, a Russian with a great sense of humour, we were doing our morning inspection tour of the rig walking over the deck he looked down at a skip full of scrap metal and laughed ,

"Hey Mike, look I see the spares have arrived."

We came up to Apollinaire, the Filipino welder, he spent all trip filling up the skips with metal, but no construction ever appeared. Yan watched him and frowned,

"I cannot figure out why he is here Mike, he has the other Filipinos around him all day having a laugh, but they never produce any work or repairs, I'm considering taking him in to the office today." I laughed "Do you mean for interrogation; we've heard all about you Russians."

We walked down to the Pump room situated in the bowels of the ship. dark and smelly condensation ran down the walls, which was really the ship's hull, it was covered with rust, the walkway was metal grating about a meter from the actual bottom of the ship, water swished from side to side it reminded me of a horror movie. I noticed the room had good ventilation, the pumps were not running so no heat, I asked Yan,

"Yan are you sure this is condensation,"

"what do you mean Mike,"

"well this rust is so bad it looks like a cream cracker,"

I picked a lump of the rust off with my thumbnail instantly water oozed out,

"maybe I should give it a tap with my adjustable spanner just to see how deep it is,"

Yan yelled,

"No please Mike no,"

I tasted the water,

"I thought so its sea water Yan, not condensation did you know that Yan, I tasted it again to be sure and yes it is sea water this hull has become porous, we should report it Yan, I think we need to check the rest of the ship if this water gets into the Bilge pump motors or the thrusters motors we will have big problems, like we did when the pirates rammed my last ship and the bilge pumps burnt out remember."

Yan pleaded,

"Mike please don't say anything, I could be fired, I should have reported it a long time ago"

I asked him,

"Are the bilge pump motors ok the salt affects them fast"

"yes, the crew fitted the spare motors,"

Yan assured me.

It turned out the severe rust was not limited to the pump room, and the decks farther along, it was so bad we wrote a report to head office, after 2 weeks there was a reply, basically there was no budget for a shipyard repair,

We were told in the report to monitor it, we included photos which showed the extent of the rotten hull. The thickness of the hull was down to a few millimetres it should have been 6mm one collision with another ship and this hull would cave in.

Drilling companies at that time tended to spend as little as possible on maintenance, with little regard for the safety of their crews. Maintenance was a necessary evil to drilling companies, they had no respect for tradesmen drilling must continue 24/7 no matter what.

It never occurred to the drilling office, that breakdowns happened due to lack of maintenance, I in my wisdom blurted this out at the next phone conference with town, clearly, they did not appreciate my input the following trip I was transferred to another ship. The "Roger Eason," which was worse, the rust was so bad I was on constant marathon changing out rusty parts for serviced ones for 12 hours a day, it was exhausting, I complained to Stafford the chief he chuckled.

"Mike lad, the drilling rig had an overhaul last year,"

"I don't see any evidence of an overhaul, it's hard to believe, Ill check the paperwork."

So I made my way down to the workshop it was a dark and silent place quite foreboding, no one ventured down there according to the store man Jo, so he and I had the lower decks to ourselves, above my office stood a huge Hi-fi system and the usual lathe, milling machine, hydraulic hose crimper, it was a large workshop, but stacked high with old flanges hydraulic cylinders and hundreds of other rusty parts that had to be constantly moved to access anything. Everything was covered with dust. The hi-fi was great the speakers were huge at least a meter by half a meter. Every day the Brazilian steward brought me fruit and cakes at break time most of the fruit was rotten, so it had to be eaten by cutting chunks off, it was full of worms and other wiggly insects. The rig was so old I was chasing my tail to keep up with the breakdowns, and preventative maintenance. I had little to do with the Marine side of the ship, that is the propulsion, and water makers, and compressors it was run by a Dutchman, called Uva, he told me how he had trouble getting spares because the company refused to pay the bribes required to get stuff through the Brazilian customs.

I email them over and over again, the engines are overdue a scheduled bottom end overhaul by 20,000 hours,"

Uva was genuinely worried about an imminent seizure.

A week later number 2 engine blew up,

I had just left Uma's office, and walked through the engine room, the two Brazilian oilers were checking the engine oil level's in the main engines, I squeezed passed them had a quick bull shit with them.

"Hey Mike, you want Brazilian woman tonight I fix for you, I know one of the girls fancies you, perhaps you can fix a day off for me," he winked with a smile.

"ok no rubbish mind" I laughed.

I opened the heavy steel watertight door stepped through and closed it. I was suddenly thrown to the deck by a large explosion the whole ship shuddered, I could see a large cloud of blue smoke pouring from the side of the ship it was the engine room, I got to my feet a bit shaken at first my ears were ringing, I struggled to open the watertight door, it was distorted, I had just closed it seconds before the explosion, I needed a hammer to move the dogs that lock the door shut, once inside visibility was not clear hot oil dripped from the roof, it was running down the walls I tripped over! It was the body of one of the oilers, I dragged him outside and cut my hand on something sharp. What I saw shocked the hell out of me I was stunned. A jagged piece of steel the size of a hand was embedded in the side of his head, I tried gently to move it, but it was stuck fast. I fell on the deck with the body of this young boy in my arms the commotion around me seemed to be unfolding in slow motion, there was an eerie silence. I was in shock I just didn't know what to say or think a feeling of despair came over me, my hands, covered with the boys blood they shook uncontrollably I felt sick, minutes must have passed by the time I composed myself.

I realised the young oiler was dead, I could not help him, people were running in and out of the engine room, they emerged carrying the body of the other oiler he was laid on the deck next to his friend. For what seemed like an age no one spoke, a mixture of anger and emotion washes over you, there are no words to describe the feelings. If I had been just seconds later leaving the engine room, I too would be dead along with the two young lads.

Is the Grim Reaper hovering over my shoulder yet again? Warning me my time is creeping closer, should I change career before it's too late.

I've had so many close calls I often wonder when my luck will run out, or there is a God After all, and he is watching over me?

An investigation revealed a bearing failure was occurring on engine number two the bearing must have been glowing red hot, which ignited soon as Oxygen was introduced when the young oiler opened the oil filler cap. The Brazilian Police left the rig two days later taking a very worried looking Uma with them, he was scared stiff,

I tried to allay his worries,

"Don't worry Uma I'll contact the Dutch Consulate; I'll come and see you soon as I get off the rig."

The drilling company tried not to get involved, so he was left in the local jail. I got off the rig a week later I went to the jail in San-Palo, Uma was in a mess the cell had a sandy floor, a bucket for a toilet, the bed consisted of a bed frame with rusty springs and no legs, on the top was a filthy old mattress with no cover, it was dark and smelly no lighting, just a small window. He had been beaten that was obvious he just burst into tears when he saw me.

"Mike Get me the fuck out of here,"

"I'll do my best Uma I will need to take some pictures of you, to show the consulate, and I am going to see the warden right now mate."

Ricardo the warden spent most of his time in the bar near the jail, he didn't give a monkeys about Uma, even though he had not been to court yet, Ricardo told me to fuck off or I would find myself sharing the cell with Uma. I recorded the conversation on my phone for my visit to the consulate. I phoned the Dutch consulate in San-Palo the Consulate was horrified after I explained the situation, he immediately got on the phone.

"ok Mike thanks for the heads up I will sort this out right now you go get Uma some food, I 'll get you a hotel when is your flight back to the UK,"

"actually, I v missed it now"

"no problem Mike I 'll sort that too, call me back once you've dropped the food off at the jail,"

Uma was so pleased.

"I've been told the Dutch consulate called here, I have one more night then the consulate will be here, I am under house arrest at the Dutch embassy thank you Mike,"

"I have asked the rig electrician to print off, also email them to the Consulate all the emails you sent to the company asking for the spares that would have prevented this from happening, it should help your case,"

There's not much more I can do mate I need to go; your consulate is getting me a hotel and a flight, so I need to call the embassy, but I'll try come back later."

I called home from the consulate, my flight was not for two days, the consulate apologised but he compensated me by putting me in first class.

The drilling company got a roasting from the Dutch Consulate and lost the Drilling contract.

Uma was released and I flew home in first class. "wow."

Uma was exonerated.

Back in the 90s Brazil was a rough lawless place as was the rest of South America Tourists were herded to chosen areas, so the violent crime wasn't too visible. Beach mugging was a favourite on the Copacabana beach, I met a number of young couples at the airport in tears, they were taken at knife or gun point to their hotel and had everything taken including passports, it was a rough time in Brazil. I decided this would be my last trip I will call Debbie and tell her, in those days, an international call required a phone card.

The hotel receptionist told me I should go and find a supermarket, they usually keep the cards by the till, I found one a short walk away, the front of the building was completely open, two concrete pillars supported the roof, I spotted the cards by the tills, As I picked up the cards, suddenly machine gun fire opened up, the bullets spattered across both pillars, debris showered over me as I fell to the floor with the other customers. I was shitting myself, I could hear shouting in Portuguese, the masked men stepped over me and dragged the till operator across the shop toward the office some ten yards away, this was my chance I saw two people get up and run so I did the same.
"fuck it"

I jumped to my feet and ran like hell down the street bullets bounced off a wall nearby showering me in plaster as I ran, I ran so hard my legs were burning I was expecting a bullet at any moment I ran and ran as I turned the corner, I could see the hotel, the bullets had stopped but I kept running, can I make it before a bullet hits me, none came I dived through the swing doors sliding across the reception area on my knees, people looked down at me quizzically like

"what the hell is this crazy person doing."
 I looked up to the receptionist struggling for breath,
"can I have my key please,"
I wheezed shakily as I got my feet, my knees were trembling they felt
weak. the receptionist smiled,
"you got your phone cards then?"
 "are you kidding there was a robbery going on, I was nearly shot,"
"Ah that was you was it, we heard the gun fire,"
she laughed.
"it happens often these days,"
"thanks for warning me then."
I was leaning on the desk now trying to get my breath back my hands
still trembled. Once in my room, I called home to say I am on my way
home and I'm not coming back here. It was just another exciting day,
or was it, I thought, I seem to get them very frequently, one day my
luck will run out, so I am not sure if that's good luck or bad luck!
What next?
That came the next trip, I went back because I had to work notice. I
was on my way home it was time to catch the chopper after a long
busy trip, I boarded the chopper and sat on the side seats at the back
next to Jo the store man, there were no doors on these old choppers,
I'm sure they were ex-Vietnam rejects it was forty minutes into the
hour of the flight, we seemed to be losing height, Jo and I looked
quizzically at each other, I twisted around to see the front view I could
see the beach in the distance, but still we became ever closer to the
clear blue sea minutes later looking around once more, I could actually
make out people on the beach, but then the engines cut out, the
chopper must have been 20 feet from the water, the pilot reversed
Pitched the blades to slow our decent the helicopter plunged into the
water, the inflatable's activated around the chopper, that was a relief at
least we won't sink too soon, I took another glance forward,
"I could swim that Jo are you coming?"
"Mike are you kidding look"
he gestured toward the water; I could see big dark shapes moving
around! I sat down
"sharks I bet"
we sat there for some time, the water was lapping at the base of my
seat, Jo moaned about the chopper drifting further away from the
beach each minute, some of the locals had climbed on to the top of the

chopper making it unstable, so an argument started, fortunately before a fight started a boat turned up and tied to the chopper, the locals climbed aboard Jo and I had to swim around the chopper to reach the boat, all I could think about was those big dark shapes beneath us. The boat dropped us off on the beach that was enough for me I never returned to Brazil.

The Grim Reaper was back!

Jobless I took care of my 4 sons while I converted the stable behind my house into a commercial kitchen, the stable floor was cobbled it had dry stone walls it was a fucking marathon, I dreaded DIY, I am so crap at it which made the whole episode a good laugh for the boys, (Samuel the eldest Matthew and Benjamin the twins the youngest Thomas hero-worshipped his brothers who watched over him at school like gods). I spent weeks trying the plastering lark ending up with plaster dykes along the base of all four walls, I gave that up and managed to fasten plaster boards to the not so square walls, in fact because of the very sloped roof and angled walls, For a laugh I covered the sloping floor with black and white tiles and trimmed them so they got larger to the far end of the room. I managed a similar thing on the roof so the room looked huge, a weird sensation as you entered the room through the 5 foot door the far wall was 7 foot high, it made you feel dizzy for a few seconds, so I fitted the kitchen units with same gradient as the floor and walls.

"Boys" I shouted

"come on into the stable"

All four of them hesitated in the doorway and fell silent for a few seconds, laughter burst forth as they all said,

"mum is going to go mad when she sees this,"

writhing around on the floor their laughter could be heard by my neighbour Charlie (an acclaimed joiner) he came over the fence to see what the fuss was all about,

"How the hell have you managed this Mike it gets bigger as you look across the room, I feel a bit dizzy,"

He laughed.

"Mike, can I be here when Diane sees s it! She's going to kill you."

"I warned her I am crap at DIY anyway Charlie it'll be you she comes running to, so you better be ready,"

Charlie's face immediately changed to a frown.

Charlie a professional tradesman and a wealth of experience at 60 years old he and his wife Isabel together with our other neighbour June she was about 70 years old very strict person, she never lived down the story of her alcoholic husband, who had died having a heart attack while he became stuck halfway out the living room window in a desperate bid to escape to the pub, she kept an eye on the boys because my wife often disappeared on holiday while I was away on the rigs.

There was an occasion while I was away, I Phoned home and Spoke to Samuel he was 12 years old the eldest son after a little chat I asked him to put his mum on.

"ok Son put Your mum on the line"

"She's not here she went on holiday yesterday"

Shocked I was not sure what to say,

"how long for?"

"don't know" he said,

"sailing I think" Sam laughed.

"So, who's there with you guys"

"No one just us four"

"Are you going to school"

"Oh yes" he said proudly

"I am in charge Ben and Matt do the cooking" (Benjamin and Matthew are the twins just eleven years old,) Thomas cleans the bathroom (Thomas is nine) June keeps coming around but we don t let her in"
Sam Said proudly.

I got off the rig and rushed home as I put my key in the front door June whisked the door open and stared me straight in the face in a very strong Scottish accent shouted,

"Michael where is the mother of your children, these boys have been alone for days, who told them to cook chips, at the age of 12 its dangerous,"

"why have they been hurt" I enquired

"no but they could have been and there're been dozens of kids running wild all over your house, it real mess I had to get Charlie to send them all home, You need to discipline the boys Michael they are wild a bit like you I'm sure."

June continued she proudly said

"Isabel and I have cleaned up the mess."

Over her shoulder I saw Charlie creeping past in the hall quietly laughing his head off as he glanced a look over my direction.

"So, you going to let me in then June I need to see the boys,"
"They r all in bed now, it 'll have to wait now it's late just wait until I see your wife."
June never liked Diane she did not agree with the way Diane treated the boys,
"far too cavalier and blasé, that woman is not a good mother"
she'd say."

The next episode with the boys was not long coming. It was nearly Xmas our little valley was frequently snowed in. All the kids in the village loved it, running riot through the one main street, of course there was no traffic of any sort, so they were all quite safe.
Bang Bang, on our huge front door guess who! Our two very portly village Bobbies who appeared to be quite frustrated they were the joke of the village no one took them seriously,
"we have had a report one of your lads has smashed a window in the vicarage,"
"ok come in the boys are here tell me all about it,"
"Can we see them one at a time"
Matthew volunteered to be the first for interrogation
"all this is a bit dramatic for a smashed window don't you think,"
Diane my wife demanded.
The fat copper did not think so,
"So how did you come to find out about it," she asked.
"I can't divulge that information Mrs. Youngman,"
 at this point we were all dying to laugh.
"Hang on a minute is this a bank job or just a broken window,"
I was getting pissed off myself now Matthew then piped up,
"I did it" he admitted.
"Ah! I knew it" the fat copper smiled,
"I'll have to write up a report,"
At this point I burst out Laughing
"Sorry,"
I said, "would you mind if I record this because no one will believe me if I just tell them about this."
"Mr. Youngman this is serious you could be charged with perverting the course of justice,"
"Ok" I asked how big this window is?"
Matthew jumped in,

"it's this big dad and no one lives there"
offering up his hands showing the size to be 2foot by 1 foot I could not believe it.

"Ok send in the other child please,"
by this point Diane had to cover her mouth to muffle the laughter, Ben had been listening at the door at the age of 11 Ben was a serious thinking child and was never afraid to say what he thought, and he didn't disappoint,
he announced clearly his thoughts very seriously,
"Matthew has told you the truth and you are treating him like a criminal so I am certainly not telling you the truth anyway, my dad will fix the window, won't you dad, don t talk to this person any more Matthew he's an idiot." at his point the twins ran off Diane could not hold it back any longer she burst out laughing as I did Sam had stayed in the background he also lost control, I could just about retain enough control to suggest the 2 coppers Leave now to save further embarrassment, once the front door was shut we all laughed even louder. Diane later called the local police station and complained as seriously as she could manage, we later received a letter of apology. Of course, Diane made it clear this was entirely my fault for letting the boys run wild. It was not me who went on holiday and left them alone that's different apparently that's woman's logic for you.

I had my friend the local gamekeeper to teach the boys how to tickle trout. One evening they placed some trout and frogs in the bath, Diane was working late that day, when she arrived home late, not wishing to disturb anyone she never turned on all the lights and carefully she stepped into the bath to take a shower, we heard the screams as she hurtled from the bathroom into the hall naked,
"what the fucks in the bath"
she screamed,
"you bastards did that deliberately."
 Sam calmly told her "mum it's just a couple of trout they r harmless you can cook them for us tomorrow, oh and the frogs are on their way downstairs."
He casually returned to bed; it was a Spare room offence for me. I received my orders in no uncertain terms I was to get a job as soon as possible, before I drove her mad, after considerable searches on my new computer (back then they were very slow) I received a call from Debbie, in the Aberdeen agency, asking if I would go to Nigeria to

cover for a Mechanic on a jack up situated a mile off the coast of Warri, I'd never been there before was my first thought, I'll give it a go anyway I could not stay home or I may be looking at a verbal whip lashing from the screaming skull, perhaps even a divorce that really scared me because I would really miss my boys we had such good fun unfortunately often at their mother's expense, I did feel bad about that but my boys always came first, which is possibly what drove her away in the end, she often seemed like she was looking for something, but unfortunately I never Listened, perhaps I was too protective of my boys I was determined to be a good father.

Nigeria

My Instructions were to meet a couple of the crew in Paris airport you can always spot a rig worker it's the bags and that fed up look! It's knowing your gonna be away for a month and you know the conditions will be utter crap the food even worse it's a given if working in Africa especially Nigeria. Two lads came up to me
"are you off to the Trident jack up mate"
"yes I am" they were scared judging by the look they gave me, no surprise really Nigeria has a reputation for violence and hostages were taken on a weekly basis they must have been as desperate as I was for a job, in fact, I'd say 99% of ex pats in Nigeria were only there because they had to be or money.
"I am Bill the electrician and Sandy here is the crane driver,"
great I thought, a bit of company to get through the Nigerian customs. A pat on the back I turned it was Donny the Scotsman from way back in Holland he seemed pleased to see me as I was to see my old mocker we talked through the flight to Lagos, got ushered through by the guards, of course Donny gave them some insults in Scottish
"I'll take that gun off you and ram it up Ya arse sonny" luckily, they didn't understand just frowned then waved his gun to clear off. I had been warned by the agency to watch it at their customs these lot often take your passport then make you buy it back the same applied to anything of value in your baggage. That is exactly what happened but we managed to buy them back cheap you feel so vulnerable when confronted by an AK 47 machine gun in the hands of a moron laughing in my face like a psychopath as if to say you British are at my mercy my god he had bad breath I nearly threw up!

I stuffed all my underwear back in the bag nearly breaking the zippier, I was so eager to get clear. Instructions included a transfer to Port Harcourt via a small plane, I noticed the rusty propellers torn seats and a strong smell of rotten fruit luckily we all sat together there was no system of seating just a mad scramble pushing and shoving of course none of the locals wanted to be seen sat next to a white man. Donny never took shit he gave as good as he got the Scottish aggressive growl had the locals cautious. The battered Fokker Friendship just about made lift off Donny and I took a big deep breath as we rushed towards the Jungle skimming the trees at the end of the runway. Bill looked a bit ashen as he saw the trees just a few feet below the wheels the flight took about an hour during which a snack was passed around the cabin of course it was fruit I was advised by Debbie to eat the fruit with a knife unless you were used to eating grubs and worms I looked around the plane at the other locals who seemed completely at home munching away spitting out the inhabitants into the tray.

"What the fuck"

Bill found out the hard way as he spat a grub onto his tray Sandy, and I laughed out loud and so did the locals "Piss off bastards"

"Bill mate watch what you say these guys will cut your throat and think no more of it"

Sandy rasped in Bills ear hoping no one would hear him. It was a relief to land at Port Harcourt all be it with a bone jarring thud as we touched down the cabin was starting to smell quite badly of something, I could not identify

"is that smell you Bill"

"no, it's not now fuck off you guys you know I'm scared of this place already I'm thinking I might go home" "You'll be fine"

I assured him we were all a bit anxious about it.

Once through the second security by that I mean paid the obligatory bribes to the customs and passport control. We had our bags grabbed from us by the local thugs, they grab your bag off you insisting they carry your bags to the transport the thugs then demand money by gun point. The company rep was there to meet us, "fucking bastards these lot just don't piss them off" Sandy cursed the two locals demanding American dollars instead of the Scottish pounds he offered them for carrying his bags 20 yards, you can't refuse them they all had a guns and one lad had a machine gun even the younger lads of early teens had weapons. Once on the bus I noticed the rack of guns situated near the driver the company rep informed us we would be in a hotel for the night by now there was about 8 of us ex pats 20 minutes later the bus drove up to a pair of huge steel gates probably twenty feet high barbed wire along the top and four armed soldiers on duty two of them had "Doberman Pincher dogs" straining on the leash nasty looking too, what a mess they'd make of you. This scene really assured us of our safety one of the ex-pats asked the rep

"what the fuck's all this for"?

"do not leave this compound everything you will need is here even women if you need drugs ask the barman as you check in, I will return tomorrow morning". The hotel was like apartments a large lounge and 3 bedrooms set off the central lounge area Bill, Donny and I were together as we checked in Harry the very hard looking barman asked if we needed any drugs or women it would be a small fee to him and then just pay the women

"So, is it just black women then?"

Bill asked laughing we all laughed except Harry of course he just told bill there were a couple of white women here, but they were crap "we all know of course white women prefer black men because we have much larger dicks than you white men wimps"

starring intensely straight into Bills eyes who quickly changed his tune

"just kidding Jimmy just breaking the ice pal"

"Oh, really will you be breaking anything else Jock" Harry laughed

"there's no ice around here Jock"

I interrupted,

"ok Bill mate,"

"let's go to the room then eat"

I leaned over the bar to Harry,

"he's not been abroad before he is a bit nervous" Laughing, Harry winked.

"Ok I'll send him our roughest bitch."

The rooms were sparsely furnished the beds were really hard not much in the way of other furniture, I dropped my bags on the floor and made for the shower, damn it was hot in this country, sweat constantly running down your back. once showered and dressed I arranged to see the lads at the bar. Anita the barmaid was a beautiful woman in her late twenties great figure legs of an athlete. of course, there was no room at the bar for more ex pats leering at the shiny black breasts bursting out the tight low cut dress, she moved across the bar smoothly knowing the attention she attracted, the heads all turned in unison just like watching a tennis match, me included.

"Beer!"

I snapped out of my fantasy to see her face not 12 inches from mine,

"Beer you want a beer"

she repeated,

"yes, please are there more women around here like you" "oh yes how many can you handle white man"

she laughed,

"you been talking to Harry"

Anita laughed

"Where's your friend the Scotsman"

"He will be a long Soon"

"his woman has been selected by Harry personally,"

"This I v got to see,"

all the ex-pats laughed.

"You shagged one of these types before Mike,"

Phil was a tall thin lad from Hull a Tool pusher

"No mate what's it Like,"

"bit like shagging a brillo pad, it's those tight curly pubes leave you with a right raw dick afterwards" he laughed

"I'm more scared of HIV Phil so I won't be participating anyway I am happily married; with four kids I wouldn't want to jeopardise that by giving my beloved a dose."

Africa at that time was rife with not only HIV but a whole collection of nasty social diseases I am pretty sure it still is I had a strange feeling about this job little did I know what the future had in store. Later that night two of the ex-pats I had not met, managed to sneak out of the compound. They returned in the morning escorted by the local police minus their wallets and passports, both had some nasty injuries they were sent home to the UK.

Nigerian hospitals are to be avoided unless you want to contract something like hepatitis, we found this out first-hand, because the Company rep for diplomatic reasons, had agreed with the local authorities that we would undergo a local medical. So off we were marched down through the filthy disgusting streets dodging rats and one rotting body, it resembled a man he was covered with rats flies the smell was eye watering, it just reminded one, life is so cheap here, we reached the Little River Hospital. Just to keep the peace we agreed to participate in a chest x-ray, a blood test, and a breath test followed by the Nigerian version of the survival course which involved us going to the port Harcourt swimming pool, where swimming trunks and towels were issued to us. Once changed and standing at the edge of the pool next to 40 or so Nigerians. I felt very conspicuous. the attendant came up to me,

"you must tread water for 1 minute then swim halfway down the pool dive down and swim under water through the red hoops, continue down to other end and back here. That was nothing to me since I had been swimming so much after having my arm wrenched out the socket couple of years ago. I used to swim front crawl 68 lengths in 30 minutes, what worried me was what horrible illness, one would contract from the very dirty water.

"Go on then Mike then mate just don't swallow any water and you'll be fine."

Donny laughed he then whispered in my ear,

"I'll not be participating, ear infection,"

he laughed.

Clearly the lads had decided I had to be the Guinea pig.

Sandy laughed,

"I'll make you an appointment with the Little River Hospital Mike don't embarrass us now,"

"your after me pal, so don't laugh."

I thought don t swallow any water just do it really fast I slipped into the water trod water as per instruction, then set off at my fastest pace which if I may say so, my crawl was quite fast down and through the hoops, sped down to the end and back and out of the pool double quick, immediately spitting to try and reassure myself I had not drunk any of this filthy water.

"Off you go, Sandy, it's a piece of piss."

He was not too happy, now all the locals were watching him expecting him to perform like I did.

"I don t think so, I'd rather go home this is crazy I am not doing it."

He shouted.

What a fool I felt because no one gave a shit he just walked off to get changed. The lifeguard I could see was making a beeline towards me as I headed off to the change shack "excuse me sir please can speak with you,"

Spinning around to face him and expecting trouble I braced myself,

"You were very good in the pool,"

He starred intensely at me eye to eye in fact he looked a little angry, so to break the tension I offered him my towel and swimming trunks, he was quite surprised at my gesture and looked bemused as he took them from me, smiling, he said

"you must teach me how to swim like you,"

"of course, I will see you tomorrow then." He left.

Donny burst out laughing,

"you looked worried their Mike were you expecting trouble, I was, so I followed you here."

Next morning, we were on our way to the heliport driving through the jungle, accompanied by our heavily armed escort of which there were 4 jeeps with heavy machine guns and 8 soldiers. At one point I was sure I heard gunfire in the distance, our convo suddenly turned off the road onto a track, 200 yards further on we stopped at a wooden shack, it was the only building to be seen,

"wait here"

the chief bodyguard told us.

"They're rounding us up for an execution, I v seen it on the telly,"
Sandy said shakily,

"what are you saying, Sandy, fuck off you idiot you're scaring me,"
Bill barked.

"sorry mate did I say that out loud?"

"it's just that Harry the bar man told me last night that there is trouble at the heliport."

It was common knowledge that terrorists hung out at the entrance waiting for ex pats to leave alone, it made an easy target for them. The grass where I was standing must have been 3 foot high, the clearing was about the size of a football pitch, it was surrounded by thick jungle, I could hear the birds and monkeys yelling at each other, my mind wondered, if I ran through this grass would I make it without getting bitten by some nasty reptile. Boy was I lucky to have been brought up in the Malayan Jungle least I would stand some chance if we had to run for it. I looked down at the long grass, I could see a female praying mantis consuming her mate, "poor bastard" glad humans don t do that, I thought in the case of humans it takes years and years for the female to consume the male. I jumped back as a large lizard snapped her up!

"Yes, justice at last."

What are the chances of witnessing that, or is it fate warning me my menace, the "Grim Reaper" is watching it gave me a feeling of impending doom? I could hear the approach of a chopper it landed in the long grass we had to board it quickly, thankfully it was a smooth uneventful flight to the rig thank god, the chopper looked like it was straight from Vietnam, no doors so that was reassuring, it still had American military markings on it. The rig was only a mile off the beach. We had a meeting with the OIM and Pusher they told us the rig had been held hostage some months prior to us coming, so our job was to get the rig ready for Drilling, the Rebels had smashed up a lot of the machines with their machine guns we all turned to look at each other and said out loud in unison.

"fuck."

Once stacked away I spent a few days finding my way around this wreck of a Jack up the rig, the weather was so hot and humid I was soaked with sweat all day. It was far worse below in the engine room and switch room all the panels had either bullet holes or dents which gave me the willys. Once again, I had stupidly put myself in the firing line, I collected the spent bullet shells from the floor, and considered if I should bail out now before trouble raised its ugly head as it often did where I'm concerned.

I walked across the main deck as the crew opened up a food container, out crawled 6 of the biggest Tarantulas I ever seen, bigger than the palm of my hand and 2 inches high and very hairy, they scared the shit out me the local lads laughed as I took a wide line around them. I stepped through the watertight doors leading down to the lower decks it was quite dark dust covered the lighting. I had to be cautious the stair was very steep or most a ladder I could barely see the steps. I made my way through to the watertight doors to the engine room and workshop it was so hot the sweat poured down my back, the machinery was falling apart, the first of which was the water maker there was water leaking from most of the connections, they had wire holding them together, This scene reminded me of a horror film, I pushed the engine room door open, two small young Nigerian lads were sat in the corner, they couldn't been more than 15 years old, the entire engine room was dark because the lights were coated with exhaust dust, as I passed the main engines I ran my hand over them a thick layer of carbon dust covered them too, there must be a leaky exhaust system. Only one engine was running it is always noisy and very hot in engine rooms usually 40 degrees plus. The two lads seemed nervous of leaving the confines of the engine room.

"Hey boys you don't have to remain here all day, go up on deck get some fresh air and a drink come back in 30 minutes,"

"you sure boss,"

"yeah go on no problem just take a break every thirty minutes."

The previous Mechanic was a Czechoslovakian a right bastard apparently, he kept these two young lads shut in the engine room all day long there was no need for it. Most of the machinery was working but only just. Held together with wire and tie wraps the engines had oil dripping from every joint, got my work cut out here I thought. Lunch was something to be dreaded although I was really hungry, the food so far had been a nightmare I could not identify any of it except cornflakes, so I had cornflakes along with the hundreds of creepy crawlies that came out of the box with the cornflakes. looking around the gallery there was a tall glass-fronted chiller the only occupant was a perfectly square crème caramel, it looked good, opening the door with great anticipation was a big mistake, the smell hit me like a hammer nausea was my first feeling as I slammed the door shut. The cooks must have been watching because they were laughing their heads off, a set up for new visitors to the rig I'm sure. The showers and toilets were a nightmare to, three of each for the entire crew of 70 persons, the smell of stale urine permeated throughout the rig it was horrible, on one occasion the crane driver, "Donny" and I were in there having a discussion, how to get it cleaned up. A young steward came in with his mop and bucket.

"Here we go this should be interesting eh Mike,"

we watched as he mopped around the toilets and seats, then proceeded to the showers then he proceeded to use the same mop in the sinks. My face must have been a picture as I yelled at the moron,

"hey, you, what the hell are you doing people wash and shave in those sinks you moron,"

The local moron stopped in his tracks; eyes wide open as he looked straight into my very angry face.

"What is wrong Mr,"

taking his filthy mop and bucket I hurled it through the door out onto the deck, the crane driver explained to the steward why I was so angry. Yes, the rig was a health hazard.

Next morning Bill and me both awoke suddenly to what sounded like gunfire there was shouting too, I thought I was dreaming, Donny shook me, he whispered,

"Mike what the fucks that?"

We were in Nigeria anything was possible rebels was my first thought "do we wait here to see what happens?"

the wait was short, the door crashed open there he was, a giant of a black man with a machine gun, we were dragged out of the cabin and headed down to the engine room and locked in with the other ex-pats. Shortly after the night shift crane driver joined us, he had a bleeding nose and swollen eye, he was close to tears. We consoled him best we could, once more the door opened the big fella with the machine gun shouted above the noise of the engine, "Mike Youngman Mechanic" of course everyone looked at me, talk about shit yourself I nearly did first thought occurred to me was they are goanna shoot me! Terrified you bet; my whole body trembled the two young oilers were with him they came over smiling.

"Come Mike, they are letting you go you were kind to us don't be scared Mike, this rig has been taken hostage before."

"I should have taken more notice of the lizard eating the praying mantis" I muttered,

Thrust on to a chopper heading for Warri, not a place to put on your holiday list, people get shot there every day apparently. The airport consisted of 4 wooden huts one of which was marked arrivals, as I walked through willing to meet a company rep. But no such luck instead there was this person wearing a uniform and peaked cap.

"You sir, please come over here I need your passport,"

I did not have it, of course, the company had it, it had been collected as we entered Nigeria. So, the official had me stay at his desk until a company rep arrived,

"I can call them if you let me go to a phone,"

"no"

was the answer,

"maybe I can use your phone,"

"no,"

he barked.

Meanwhile another chopper had arrived an expat walked by the desk,
"you"
 the official barked,
"I need your passport now"
This guy was a Dutchman a race of people I've had the pleasure of working with in the past, they don't take shit easily, the Dutchman replied loudly,
"I don t have it on me we hand them to our employers as we arrive in Nigeria, you should know that,"
The official then insisted he wait along with me at the desk.
"That's daft the Dutchman insisted, he must let us call someone he went over to the uniformed moron who after a few seconds pushed the Dutchman aside, and cursed him, he turned to me and told me to go and find a rep.
Once outside the hut, there was just a rough track with several wooden buildings down either side.
"What the hell do I do now?"
 Suddenly behind me a loud voice,
"you need a bodyguard white man,"
I spun around a very large black man stood towering over me,
"fifty dollars American I will help you."
That seemed more than fair of course trouble was I had nothing, so I rushed back inside and borrowed it from the Dutchman, I handed it over to the bodyguard, he smiled he knew I had no other option,
"I am Mohamed,"
 He smiled as he pointed down the track,
"this way."
 He had a beer in every bar we entered, until the fourth, a female voice echoed out as we took our third step,
"you must be Youngman Mike, come and have a beer with me and then we can have a fun time in my office what you think white boy."
She was huge, taller than me and a lot wider that filled me with dread, but that's not how it goes in the movies, its usually a fit bit of stuff, sadly this is reality. I told her the situation and that we had no time for fun
"Mr Mike, you don't like us black women do you; I promise you we are far better in bed than boring white women or are you scared of us."

74

She was clearly quite a confrontational person goading me for an argument. I was not going to be pushed into an argument about race for sure.

I lied; I have many black girlfriends at home I am happily married with 4 kids. We left the bar after a few beers the bodyguard followed us up to the airport, he tapped me on the shoulder handed me a bullet "see you later white man,"

he crossed the track and disappeared into the jungle. I looked at the bullet in my hand, his name was scratched on it. Annie the rep looked and smiled,

"he liked you, Mike, if he did not that is the bullet, he would have shot you with,"

For some reason that really scared me, she had a chat with the official then confidently she escorted us around to the fixed wing flights, we were soon flying back to Lagos.

"Do not leave the airport wait until you are picked up," was our instructions, as if I would, where the fuck would I go. After a 2 hour wait the ride turned up in a bulletproof 4x4, the driver had guns all around him, he had a pistol at his side and a machine gun clipped next to his seat, as did the co-driver not very reassuring. 30 minutes of navigating the many large potholes in the road the 4x4 pulled into a safe house. 20-foot walls all around it had broken glass scattered along the top, two soldiers patrolled it with Doberman pincher dogs for company sounds secure, but what scared me was that it was normal here it was a very large house. The huge electric gates opened the house was a modern build looked very posh. A well-dressed black woman met us at the door, she was quite a glamorous woman and certainly knew how to dress to please the eye, she eyed us both up smiled a knowing smile, her hips swayed as she moved.

"My name is Ruby,"

"who is Youngman Mike," she looked directly at me,

"you,"

"Yes, I am why,"

"I had a call to say you were coming, I had a call from the Trident, to watch out for you, my son works on that rig in the engine room, dinner in 2 hours, a woman will be sent up to your rooms shortly."

She smiled.

I had to laugh the Dutchman (Rudi was his name) asked me,

"what's so funny Mike?"

"you couldn't make this up, could you Rudi?"

He laughed.

The room was very large as was the bed, there was a TV there was not a channel to be had. The bed was hard as a rock, the bathroom was nice and clean too. I found all the toiletries I needed. I jumped in the shower in time to hear a loud knock on the door, I answered it wrapped in a towel.

"Hello Youngman," she smiled,

"you won't be needing the towel tonight, well maybe later."

She was so black I could hardly make her out in the dark hallway, once she stepped through the door what a sight, there stood the most beautiful girl I had ever seen, but very young perhaps 16/19, I sat her down on the balcony, I was about to step in to the shower a thought suddenly shot into my mind, she is very likely going through my few things right this minute, so I darted out and sure enough she looked up surprised holding on to my wallet, she dropped it,

"I sorry Youngman,"

"It's just Mike, and don't worry about it what's your name."

Her name was April she spoke good English, I decided to take her in the shower with me, then we could have a beer and talk. It turned out she had been sold to a human trader by her parents, the family were starving, she was ten years old then, for years she was a slave to some Nigerian drug baron, it is common practice and still is today. As April got more beautiful, she was forced to do sexual favours for clients of the Drug Dealer, he was later shot by a rival. It chance for her and several other girls to escape, they stuck together and now work for an escort agency servicing ex pats. I asked Ruby to send dinner for two up to the room. We talked for hours before retiring to the dreaded hard bed which thanks to April I soon forgot.

It's such a corrupt system in Africa and I can't see it ever changing, Charity has been pouring into Africa for decades it has not made any difference the level of poverty I witnessed really disturbed me.

No one collects the garbage there are huge stacks of rubbish higher than the buildings and rotten the smell is awful, yet I saw the level of desperation as dozens of women and children picked through the rotten stinking garbage for a morsel of food. I came across several dead bodies strewn across the gutter in one street they were crawling with insects, rats fought over the fresher bits of the bodies. When it rains the streets flood within minutes 12 inches of filthy brown water flows into the dwellings along with the garbage and rats.

Before I left I gave April what was left of Rudi's money, Rudi and I were picked up an hour later and taken to the airport, on the way there the traffic was gridlocked so our driver, not wanting us to miss our flights ordered our escort to clear the road (this was a jeep with 4 armed soldiers) who promptly started threatening the motorists blocking our path by pointing their ak47s at them, shots were fired into the air that had us hiding down behind the rear seats, a few moments later we continued on our way. Once we reached the airport, I saw the company rep outside holding a sign above his head with my name on it, I leapt from the jeep,

"you got my passport and ticket?"

"Yes, sir I have."

I was so glad, I grabbed it and darted for the departure gate I swore to myself never to return. I never meet Rudi again of course, once home I told my wife the story, but I am sure she thought I was making it all up. My boys were fascinated especially the bit about the praying mantis eating her mate my son Sam said

"Dad you better watch it mum might try doing that to you"

"she is son, but it takes years and years"

we all laughed.

The images I saw have stuck in my mind ever since, the poverty was sickening the visions of the children picking through garbage to find their next meal, Dead bodies in the street were commonplace just like an abandoned car it's just another reminder of what their future holds! Nothing!

"Knock Knock God you watching"?

"I don't think so!

After a long stretch at home and the Nigerian incident still fresh in my mind like a recurring nightmare, the thought of going away offshore had lost is an appeal. So far, my oil career had been somewhat tainted with danger potential life-threatening incidents fortunately for me other people's I consider myself very lucky.

some sort, does this occur wherever the oil industry works or am I what's known as a Jonah? I kept up to date with Rig zone news on the internet there were other incidents of course but few like mine so I felt a little reassured maybe our God up there did have it in for me or is he there watching over me? They say "you need faith" but faith has to be earned.

God, are you listening"?

We lived in a small village in the beautiful Scottish borders a shop, Petrol station and the Bank that's it and all at the gates of Ayton castle. The gates formed part of the main street the only other feature was the river Eye water flowing down through the castle grounds to the port of Eyemouth.

There was only farmland visible in the distance, during harvest season the Farmers employed the local population, so we all knew each other even the three schoolteachers joined in. Once a month we had the family trip to Edinburgh on one occasion the boys were having the usual dispute over who sat at the window seat normally Ben had a window he had learnt that if he feigned sickness,

"Mum, I feel sick"

his three brothers immediately squashed up together away from him giving him the space he wanted. I could see in my wing mirror the sneaky smile of victory on his face. So, one day a gypsy woman and her kids were passing our front door selling wooden pegs, my wife did not tolerate fools or begging so the woman was told to be on her way. Not me the Soft touch I bought some pegs she looked at Ben closely he has small circle of white hair on the back of his head, she caressed his head softly,

she whispered straight to my face.

"this child has been blessed by god you will never have to worry about him,"

She was right Ben has been very lucky since that day his life has been a blessed one, it just seems to go his way; he is now 37 a highly paid subsea supervisor.

My life has been an upward struggle, I've always had to work hard to progress through life.

France

A Month later I was on my way to Brest to assist a commission a new semi-sub rig.

Thousands of workers were involved from many countries and after a week of constant arguments over jobs and the way to carry them out, progress was slow the project fell far behind schedule. from my perspective the only folk who got on were the Brits, Dutch and the Canadians. It was chaos from the start all the drawings were in French, so all us foreigners were fucked. I marched off to the operations office, A large crowd had gathered at the operations office all speaking different languages all at the same time, all directed at one very stressed French Engineer called Xavier, people thrusting the drawings in his face he shouted frantically,

"I can do nothing; I don't make the drawings up."

He then retreated into the inner office and shut the door, the rabble all looking at each other as if to say,

"what the fuck do we do now,"

"coffee anyone,"

I announced,

"good idea," someone yelled above the mela, they were all gone as if by magic, I waited for a few minutes more, Xavier slowly sneaked out of his hiding place,

"what the fuck do you want?"

"Are we getting drawings in English,"

"no."

He stepped back through the door, reappeared with some drawings then scurried off between all the containers. and vanished.

I followed the rabble to the coffee shop the coffee shop, it was just a bus shelter with vending machine, the dock authority, under pressure by the crews, inserted the vending machine into it at the last minute. One Morning I was inspecting the high-pressure pipe work for the Mud pumps it seemed to be progressing faster than the planning report, I noticed the French welders were not preheating the high-pressure piping before welding it. If high pressure pipe (thick walled) was not pre-heated it could lead to cracks in the weld, it was dangerous so of course, I had to report it.

A day or so later several Dutch welders arrived with instructions to take over from the French, but the French had not been informed and were not happy. The dispute between the welders escalated into a brawl, it required the dock security and an ambulance to treat several French welders.

The Dutch are big by nature and do not take shit from anyone, I know having worked with them on many occasions, whereby the French are governed by their emotions they are quick to react if they feel insulted, let's call it human nature.

I believe it is human nature which will likely be the cause of the downfall of the civilised world.

The Rig called the "Sedco Express" was state of art but it did have its teething problems, the locker room and toilets showers sinks shelves were all stainless steel somebody had done a great job fitting the Lockers toilets and sinks, long wooden benches stretched along the locker room it was a great job many of us sat in there for coffee and a bull shit.

I was on my way to the galley for lunch if you weren't French you had to be first in line if not, you ate your lunch on the stairs. The French filled the Galley and sat there the whole 2 hours the galley was open. So that's why I took the short cut through the locker room. As I passed through an over powering smell had me cast my eye around for the source, I could see lumps of human excrement all over the walls and toilets it had been smeared by hand you could tell by the five brown trails leading up to each lump I felt ill. The French camp boss burst through the door and looked around the room, a dagger stare came directly at me, I laughed,

"don t look at me mate," he swore for a good 10 minutes while he inspected the room. Michele was a slightly built man fine featured he was quite effeminate and way too much tan, I've seen it before on Brits who over tan and become a funny shit colour. I decided to have a laugh,

"you will never get the stewards to clean this up, in fact I would not be surprised if they'd quit rather than clean this up maybe someone has a grudge against you Michele."

He looked at me I could swear a tear ran from his eye,

"Mike you could help me."

I told him I had to go, there was no way I was getting too close to this mess the smell was bad enough.

"Mike, I had two Moroccan men asking for jobs yesterday I sent them away but before they left, a curse was put upon me by them,"

"how do you know that?"

I laughed,

"One of them chanted a prayer then made pointing gestures at me I am a marked man Mike" he cried.

His thin bony hands were trembling as he leant against my shoulder.

"This is an Oscar winning performance Michele."

I started to consider helping him but then the door opened,

"it is them,"

Michele Screamed,

he dropped kicked one of them, the second tried to hide behind me, so I punched his solar lexis hard, down he went, Michele's display of martial arts was impressive,

"now you two fairies'," he barked in a screechy voice,

"Clean this up, do a good job I Might get you a position as a steward,"

he winked at me and walked out, I followed him out smiling. Minutes later he was serving food in the galley dressed in the same clothes he was wearing in the locker room. I later came down with sickness and the shits believe me it was bad I had to go home.

The next year brought big changes to my family, my wife decided she wanted to live in Spain permanently. Over the last few years, I had invested all my hard-earned cash buying a house in the Costa del sol, since my pensions were making no profit at all I cashed them in to fund the house in Spain. My boys had joined the Army how I missed them but not as much as my youngest son Thomas, he looked so forlorn the day his brothers left, I could have cried he was alone for the first time he looked up to them so much . It seemed an age since the days we spent in my garage restoring vintage motorcycles teaching my sons how they worked. I built small motocross bikes for them to blast around the fields near the house, it grew into a small club, the boys bringing their mates and their bikes to my workshop for a repair or a service then the lot of them would blast off to the fields. Of course, they all ended up good motorcyclists, we actually taught my wife to ride too. Later the older three joined the Army, they were based in Germany. They rarely came home on leave but when they did it was not always convenient for their mother who preferred to be in Spain at our holiday home in the countryside, she had sent Thomas off to live with his girlfriend's family he was only too happy. This was the difference between me and her, while we were at Pepe Alba (the house name) I was constantly worried about the boys whereas she never seemed to be bothered, it really bugged her, me phoning Sam to make sure they were all ok especially as the Iraq war was looming and their Regiment was sure to go. Diane and

I were drifting apart she would often go on walks with her two boxer dogs and be gone for hours, I frequently found her down at the local bar enjoying the attention paid to her by the Spanish and Romanian men, she was the only woman amongst 20 men. The rot had set in I had seen it before, I had to put it out of my mind, my imagination ran wild as I walked back to the house without her, she preferred the attention she received at the bar. I had to get away and put all this worry behind me, shortly after she asked me for a divorce.

"leave me with this house and ill not ask for more," she lied.

We split up, I bought another house for me and my four boys in the UK. A year later it was Christmas Eve I was alone in the house the boys were out with girlfriends celebrating, Matt called me,

"Dad what are you doing on your own at Christmas?"

I could hear talking in the background he came back

"Dad, Vickie's (Matt's girlfriend) Mum is on her own too why don t you go and see her?"

"Oh yes, Matt, a stranger knocking on her door asking her on a date, out of the blue oh yes that will work,"

"Vicky has told her mum about you dad, so off you go."

I had to laugh my lads trying to fix me up, but it was touching too. I did go and see her, she must have thought I was as mad as a box of frogs, she opened the door there stood before me was Vicky's mum not quite what I was expecting she was very pretty, slender legged with a warm smile,

"you must be Mike, I've heard all about you or should I say warned,"

I smiled

"I have Wine fancy a drink."

"great opening line Mike you might at least ask my name no, I'll save you the trouble, its Karen."

"clearly Mike you're not the romantic type you better come in."

At this point I was sure if I'd blown it. I could tell she was nervous, so I tried to assure her my intentions were strictly on the level, she laughed,

"who are you kidding, you 'll need to do better than that like I said I have been warned, I know what your boys are like and I can see where it comes from now."

We had a rocky start mainly due to my rather tactless way I had three current passports at that time which, when Karen saw them lying on the dresser, they were all current so she thought I was a spy at first, so

I played along for a short time by refusing to tell her where I'd been and what I did for a job. After a few years she took the plunge and moved in with me I was honoured, we v been together ever since.

That dreaded day arrived with news no parent wants to hear.

Matthew called me, he told me they were off to Iraq, and that the equipment they had been supplied with was rubbish, and in short supply, such important things like body armour and desert boots Helmets, and uniforms, I flew back home and bought £1000 worth of kit, I drove to Fallingbostel, in Germany, to make sure they got the kit before the regiment left for the shipyard. it was an illegal war and Tony Blair lied to gain support for it as we all know there were no Weapons of mass destruction. I sent him an email from the 10 Downing street website.

"You are sending my sons to an illegal war if anything happens to them, remember I know where you live."

The one and only reply read,

"Please stop emailing us,"

At least it was something. Wouldn't it be nice if one got a reply from God, least, we would know he was there, all we have are rumours and a book?

"Are you really here God? I have doubts mate!"

"There is much suffering down here and we are making it worse by the day."

China.

Shekou town, hell it was hot and humid and very smelly, I could not figure out what the smell was, let's just say it reminded me of a septic tank I once cleaned out on a defunct Jack up rig. What the hell was I doing there? well a good friend at a well-known agency asked me if I watched James Bond Movies,

"I love them,"

"I am so glad to hear that Mike because we need a mechanic out in China ASAP. It's a last-minute thing we will arrange the visa once you're in Hong Kong, you will be met at the airport by an agent he will arrange a hotel for you and the ferry across to China. It's good money too, we're sending you a Mobile phone it will be with you tomorrow it's so you can keep in touch with us.

"Ok then email me the details and flight, a mobile phone you say, no gun? Seriously, Bond had one?"

I laughed.

"Here I go," I thought another exciting day!

After 2 hours waiting at the Burger bar in Hong Kong airport, I decided to use the Mobile phone they gave me,

"emergencies only," the note on the phone said, as I pulled it from the box, then a thought struck me.

"Why the phone they v never given me one before why now?"

Debbie answered, "I have been sat here for 3 hours now and no one has turned up, the airport police are giving me dirty looks,"

"ok" she said

"I'll make some calls."

An hour later a china man turned up, by this time I was so sick of cheeseburgers I've never eaten one since,

the china man enquired

"Mr Mike,"

"I am that man,"

I replied,

"I will take you to Canton road, please come to my taxi," I was dropped off at the Golden lion Hotel, it was very posh and guess what! There was no booking for me! Immediately I was on the phone again,

"Debbie what the hell is going on,"

I was tired after a long flight and suppressing farts from eating too many burgers it was becoming embarrassing.

"Mike, we are sorry you should have been told, a man called Richard Woo, will come to meet you there, he will sort it all out. You can't miss him he has a bad Limp, and a very large scar across his cheek,"

"you been reading too many books Debbie, love this is reality not a Bond film,"

"I am serious Mike, why do you think you were asked if you liked Bond movies,"

she laughed.

"I'll give it an hour then I am booking myself in here."

Ten minutes passed, and there he was, shuffling his way through the crowd at the very busy reception area, He was a very thin man he had a very bony face, the scar was so bad you couldn't miss it, the scar ran all the way from his lip to his ear, his large black rimmed glasses were far too big for his small face. He must have been in his thirties, he stood out from the crowd but not because of his affliction, but his white cloth slacks and blue blazer finished off with a white straw hat, and walking stick a real throwback from the fifties.

"You must be Richard please sit down let's have tea,"

"Oh, thank you mister Mike,"

"I must say Richard this is all very cloak and Dagger."

Richard's English was good.

"Well Mike we have no letter of invitation for a Chinese visa so I will have to use other means to obtain one for you so please keep a low profile once you arrive in Shekou."

Alarm bells started ringing in my head, he went on

"It may take me a couple of days to get one, you will have to let me have your passport of course"

"Are you kidding Richard, I am not handing my passport over to a complete stranger especially to a man with a limp and white straw hat" I laughed.

"You are a funny man Mike, but it is the only way otherwise you may be stuck here for a month before you get the visa and of course you will not be able to leave here without an exit permit,"

"so, it's a rock and a hard place is it, Richard, you give me your passport, and driving licence, get me a good hotel so I can get some sleep, oh and your phone number too please."

He smiled at me exposing his several bright gold teeth,

"I could say the same to you Mike, but if I don't agree we could be here all night,"

He handed them over along with an A4 sheet of rice paper, I filled in my details, careful not to rip it, it was very thin. I spent 4 days in that hotel it was great, I had to put everything on the bill, Richards agency would foot the bill.

"Anything you like Mike, Chinese women very sexy, you should try one we pay; no worry Mike, please enjoy now because once you are in China it not as nice as Hong Kong."

The waiter was very helpful. I wolfed down a dish called Nazi goring and slept through until nine am, I decided to have a wander around and get to know Hong Kong, It is so busy the streets are so full of people, you spend your entire time dodging people and rats, the gutters are full of rats they are as big as cats they were not fazed at all by the millions of humans passing them by, in fact, I trod on a few by accident while dodging the people, there is likely more rats in Hong Kong than anywhere I v ever been.

There are traders along the pavements selling birds and rodents fresh from a rotisserie mounted on a 3 wheeled cart, once eaten the bones are spat out into the gutter feeding the rats. In contrast, the shopping malls are raised above the pavement by a short staircase, very modern spacious and clean but most of all no crazy crowds to dodge.

A couple of days and I was bored stiff, my legs aching from the many miles I'd walked around the little streets and shopping malls all the same selling the same stuff, On one occasion, in a bar just off Canton road as soon as I sat at the bar this lovely Chinese woman sat down next to me, she clearly worked there she ordered a bottle of champagne for me,

"Hey, I don t want that"

I said

"You must," she whispered, "it is the way here."

"is it well I am out of here then,"

"you will have to pay first,"

"what for,"

"the champagne,"

"It's not opened yet," I laughed,

I could see a heavy moving my way to cut me off from the exit, but I beat him to it, he was a fat sod I easily outran him down the street. That evening I was out for a drink and a wander around the street markets, a stall was just a rug spread over the pavement the merchandise is anything from watches to jewellery or women, all the traders were Africans. The local traders hated them for cheapening the industry at one time these markets sold good quality stuff, but now it seemed to be junk and dodgy electrical goods.

I heard shots fired and police sirens, people were running down the street I tried to see what the trouble was, as the chaos subsided a short cautious walk and the cause of the commotion was right in front of me, two black Africans lying bleeding in the road from gun shots it looked like a bungled robbery.

A little Chinese policeman ushered me away

"catch them red hand eh,"

"oh yes we were waiting," he smiled smugly.

"African bustards'" he muttered.

Next morning, I meet Richard down at reception.

"Mike, at last, I have the visa, but you have to go tonight on the ferry to Shekou then please take a cab to the Ming Waa hotel, it is all

86

booked for you, I will take you to the ferry please go get your case, the ferry terminal is under the posh shopping malls on Canton road it is very busy and there are Chinese police watching, but don t worry about them Mike, but there is a security check at the end of the trip."

"Sounds cloak and dagger Richard, why the secrecy with this simple trip I'm just a Mechanic least I was last time I checked, I hope I am not getting in over my head here, I really don t want to end up in a Chinese jail Richard, I think you better tell me now or I am out of here."

"You cannot Mike, you do not have an exit permit," "When do I get that?"

"I have asked for one it should be here in a week I will send it to the drilling office in Shekou, Bobby Loo is the boss he will call you when he has it."

It was clear I had no choice.

"Richard why all the sneakiness with my entry into China, I am not moving until you tell me,"

I insisted, Richard was very nervous, I could tell from his nervous trembling fingers on the arm of the chair he insisted I never tell anyone I knew what he was about to say.

"Better get a drink Richard I can see you are scared; my alarm bells are ringing something is not right is it mate?"

"It Is a Triad matter they are the dominant mafia in Shenzhen province, and they have good friends in the local Government the Triads are ruthless and often murder people they want to have their own people on the rigs, so eventually they will have some control of the oil, a list of positions has been made up for their people to fill but they are not happy with the positions. The triads want their people in higher grade jobs than the list has stated, so COSDC has told them they will see how many positions are available, so we need to fill the vacancies ASAP but in a way the Triads will not realise it was done before the list was made, if we had got your visa the normal way they would know you were coming and stopped your visa."

" Oh, I see" I replied, so when they find out who I am, I'll get Bumped off so their guy can have the position as a mechanic. I am going home right now, I'll go see the British Consulate first and when I get back to the UK,"

I was well pissed off and scared, how easily I'd been set up into this mess. I called Debbie at the office in Aberdeen she was horrified, "we knew nothing of this Mike stay at the hotel until I sort this out, put Richard on the phone please,"

I spent the next few days getting pissed and sleeping most of the day away, the TV was crap of course, it was all Chinese, however, a call from Debbie brought me back to the here and now.

"We need you to go mike, I can assure you; you will be safe I have changed your position on the rig list maintenance manager!"

I laughed,

"you will get £1000 a day, we pay the tax and all expenses, if it works out you will get a bonus because we will have a soul contract to supply all the expat personnel to this contract."

"What is the risk rushed through my mind and imagine 28k tax free, "I'll do it."

I heard myself say, I felt so cheap.

Richard was at my door the next morning

"Hey Mike, I have your ferry ticket please to come you need to get the next boat."

Once on board I looked around for another white man, I spotted one sat on his own. Freddy was from Finland he was a Nokia Mobile phone rep; he was a real comedian making constant comments about the Chinese.

"Freddy, not a good idea mate, what if these guys understand English, they're not gonna be Very happy with you mate,"

I told him.

I showed him my company phone because it was a Nokia,

"wow! that's the latest thing Mike, only a few select people get those, these are very expensive you must be an important man Mike."

That just fuelled my suspicions of something fishy going on. We reached the security at Shekou, I was behind Freddy in the queue the Chinese guards were all chattering away the queue was moving slow it came to Freddy's turn. He was quickly whisked away to a little room I could see the look of horror on his face as he looked around, the door slammed shut. That was worrying just my luck bet it'll be my turn next. It wasn't I got through fine no check, I just walked through which was strange because everyone apart from myself had their bags opened, I thought perhaps Richard had contacts here. I waited outside for Freddy, a good twenty minutes later out he came walking with a limp, he's been beaten up I thought.

"No, I just had a fucking internal, Mike it really hurt you were right I should have shut up on the boat my arse is fucking sore,"

I had to laugh.

"I 'll not be nursing you, Freddy, come on let's get to the hotel. The Ming Waa Hotel was at the top of a hill overlooking the town centre, it was the tallest building in town, maybe 30 stores high quite modern and quite busy. Fortunately for us there was two receptionists that spoke good English, so checking in was a breeze, there were not so many Expats working there at that time the oil industry was still young and in the dark ages. The next morning my bones ached badly talk about hard mattresses, the Chinese have it covered mine had no give at all I met the other ex-pats at breakfast the tool pusher introduced himself.

"Hi, you must be Mike, I am Tom, we are all working down at the "Chi One shipyard so just tag along,"

"Jim the spark will keep an eye on you for now."

So, we paraded off in single file the pavements are narrow, and the traffic was so dangerous you had to keep well clear of the road. We took the local bus.

"there were two services a slow one and a fast one,

Jim smiled.

"Mike never take the fast service they are very dangerous they crash most days you can tell which is which only by the number of dents and scraps on the body work."

On the route I saw women on their knees fitting cobblestones into the road using just a hammer. All day long they were there every day hammering stones into the papered surface. It's the women in China that build the roads it seems, not Only that, but they build a better-quality road than the UK roads. I settled in the yard quickly helping overhaul top drives. After a week or so I noticed four guys in light Blue coveralls and straw hats squatted in the corner, they never lifted finger I called over the interpreter Soy Lyn pointing at them, I said,

"see those guys over there with the flat straw hats what is their job why do they just sit all day,"

"No Mike do not annoy these guys they are Triads very bad people,"

it was too late one of them got up and sauntered over toward me. My first instinct was to run but I thought no I shouldn't show I am scared, I was actually bricking it he looked a right evil-eyed twat, I readied myself for a fight, 6 inches away I could smell his breath his eyes were piercing mine but I held my nerve, and glared back then I had a horrible realisation he may pull a knife what do I do then die? I guess running would have been a better option I thought.

"you have a problem Mister Mike?"

"yes, I do why are you not helping the guys who are working?"

"That is easy Mister," he replied,

"not our job, our job is fix problems you have problem with someone Mister we fix for you what you in UK call bodyguard,"

"so, you are a bodyguard then," I smugly replied,

"that's right and if you don't shut up you will need one OK!"

he laughed and returned to his mates all laughing at the stupid Brit I was pissed off I walked over,

"all you guys speak English?"

"Yes, we do" came the reply.

"How about I pay you three to beat up this guy,"

I said pointing to the Triad who I had just spoken with, the triad in question stood up,

"Here we go" I thought crossed a line

"I like you, Mike you are a funny man,"

The thug removed his course straw hat and placed on my bald and very sunburnt head, which hurt, believe me, I could feel the blood running down the back of my head from the cuts inflicted by the course straw hat, but I could not show weakness, we all had a laugh and I made a swift exit nursing my bleeding head.

Soy Lyn and I became good friends over the next few weeks, However One morning he looked quite worried he was very quiet later he came to me.

"Mike can you fix cranes, my friend is in trouble,"

"Yes, I can mate why,"

"my good friend woo is the driver here down at the quayside, there is a ship coming in, it has Triad cargo if he cannot unload it, they will beat him,"

"Fuck sake,"

I thought

"why do I constantly get involved in people's problems wherever I go,"

"Yes, of course, I will have a look when is the ship due to come in?"

"It is in two hours please we must hurry mike."

So we ran down to the quayside and climbed up the crane where I found, "Timsan," the operator he was in tears with fear poor man, I felt quite sorry for him I eyeballed the engine it was old and a mess, it had not had attention for ages that was clear, the air filter housing was a large square metal box, I could see the filter was really old and bent in toward like a dinner plate, clearly it was blocked I prized it out then fitted the cover.

"run it without the filter it 'll be fine crank it over"

it started fine Timsan was very happy, I could tell from the hugging and kissing. I never had the heart to push him off and tell him it's not macho in the UK to be seen hugging another man.

Soy lyn shouted,

"the boat I can see it we must go the triads will be here,"

we rushed down the ladder and ran behind some containers, sure enough 5 minutes later 2 stretched limos drove up with a truck following in behind. It was like a movie these guys stepped out black suits dark glasses real mean looking fuckers there was eight of them 6 of them had guns! The precious load was landed on the truck strapped down and they left. Timsan ran over babbling in Chinese Soylyn translated for me,

"he said thank you,"

"Mike, these are bad men, even the police do not cross them, I will repay my debt to you one day."

Two days later I am approaching my hotel room and squatted by my door is a young girl chatting at me in Chinese, she tried to follow me into the room, I pushed her out a few times, she pushed back before bursting into tears. Puzzled I took her down to the reception girl Chan, to get her to explain, it turned out Timsan the Crane driver had given me his 15-year-old daughter, shocked, I protested it must be some mistake in the interpretation, I was assured several times by the head receptionist there was no mistake.

"It is law in China, families can only have one child and most want a son to carry on the family name."

I protested,

"That is not right it should not be allowed it's a crazy law,"

"what am I to do with her,"

Chan said firmly, straight at my face like she was angry,

"take her home,"

I laughed, "oh yeah my wife will be fine with that,"

The girl was in floods of tears she clearly got the jest of the conversation,

Chan continued very irate,

"if you return her, then her father will throw her out into the street, he will believe she has not pleased you, she will end up a beggar or in a home which is worse, please keep her Mr Mike, she can stay here with you; we will give her work while your away."

Dumbfounded, I decided to discuss it with Gerry, the Aussie electrician, he was around my age, a very easy-going man, I found him in the restaurant, once I'd explained my dilemma, he burst out laughing,

"Mike how do you do it, you get yourself in these Pickle's, all this as well as your situation with the triads your gonna meet a sticky end I'd stay home if I were you Mike,"

"It happens to me all the time Gerry, maybe I will,"

"we heard you've got a bit of a reputation Mike, the oil industry is a small world your reputation precedes you, I was warned when we knew you were coming, keep Mike on the straight and narrow we were told."

Nye Soon was her name, every evening when we returned from the yard, we'd find her waiting at the door of the hotel, she would bow to us and call me master, I soon stopped that,

"Nye I am not your master you will call me Mike and he will be Gerry, ok,"

She looked to the receptionist who translated then nodded, we sat down to eat, Nye-soon sat cross-legged on the floor in the corner, I picked her up and sat her on a chair at the table,

"you will eat with us ok,"

I pointed to the chair she nodded,

"Mike, she does not understand a word you're saying,"

Chan the receptionist was stood behind me laughing,

"Mike, we taught her to say, "yes master" just today",

"I will explain to her what you have tried to tell her"

"Better still as part of our deal I will keep her, but you must teach her English while I am at work,"

Chan, smiled, "ok Mike but you must take her with you when you leave, you will require papers for her."

"More problems,"

I looked at Gerry, and frowned,

"shit Gerry talk about rock and a hard place we better get on it now,"
I later contacted the British consulate, but as I expected they were not interested. Gerry tried the Aussie consulate, they were very helpful, within a month, we had secured papers so she could go to Perth, with Gerry, his wife had a small shop, he was sure his wife would look after her.

The next morning, I was cornered by the four Triads the moment I walked through the yard gates,

"Mr Mike, you are leaving us soon, we hear you are taking Nye Soon with you is that right?"

"What's it to you guys?"

"We will take her, she can sell flowers and sex in the bars and make us money, we have many girls who do this,"

"No way" I told him,

"I have met these girls, in fact I saw one of them beaten, she was dragged from the bar Gerry, and I were drinking in, she was beaten for not making enough money for your Colleagues, they warned me not to interfere or I would get the same treatment, is this the Chinese way?"

"For women yes, it is Mike, you take her then good luck, but if you come back here, we will cut your throat."

he screamed, then he was gone.

I never did get his name, Gerry took her to Perth, Nye soon now works in his wife's shop so a happy ending for all of us. Especially for me, the Triads scared the shit out of me, the evil looking bastards. There were times I had visions of my throat getting slit.

Sakhalin

A month on the dole followed that little treat in China a cruel society for a woman.

A call from another agency in Aberdeen asking if I would be interested in filling in on a platform in Russia. A place called Sakhalin Island. Described as "hell" by Anton Chekhov. Located at the far eastern end of the Russian Federation, just north of Japan, Sakhalin Island was where imperial Russia, once sent some of its most unfortunate convicts, a journey that was usually one-way. In Soviet times it became a closed military base; site of the notorious shooting down of Korean Air Lines flight 007 after it strayed over Sakhalin in

1983. If you visited this island 10 years ago and compare it now, you would see a big, big improvement, Once arriving in Moscow It's a 2 day journey to reach Nogliki, my destination, starting with a twelve hour flight from Moscow followed by a night in Yuzhno the largest city in Sakalynisk then it's off to the station for the 14 hour train journey to Nogliki, followed by an overnight stay, Nogliki or Nivkh's word *noghl-vo* which means "smelling village". Around 1000 people live there. It's one of the main population centres for the Nivkh tribe it is 613 kilometres north of Yuzhno. It was like going back in time fifty years, there is nothing there it is barren and it is such a harsh environment temperatures of minus 50 and ten feet of snow most of the winter which lasts for 10 months, you can only admire the people for their resilience and determination.

The train trip took 14 hours the train carriages were just like we had in the UK back in the 50's/60's, separate cabins brass rails ran down the side of the windows the entire carriage was lined with real wood, it could have been a replica of the trains I'd seen in war movies. I could imagine myself as the spy in the film, "The 39 steps", as I watched out the window of my tiny train compartment, I had fortunately had to myself, for the first two hours I watched the ever-deepening snow. The daylight lasts 4 hours but there is nothing to see just snow. The cabin was so small I could touch both sides with both arms outstretched, it was complete with a table and narrow beds either side of the table, if you tried a half turn on the bed you will end up the floor as I did. The drilling company had generously furnished me with a carry out consisting of tea bags sandwiches, a pot noodle and two tins of beer, Pure luxury! At the end of the car was a small pot belly stove watched over by the hostess who lived in a cabin adjacent to the stove. I had been advised to carry a 3-foot length of cord to tie the cabin door shut before sleeping. Stories of sexy women wondering the train looking for trade were rife, if their trade was slow long slender arms felt around the cabin door and slipped into the pockets of any clothing hanging by the door. Passports are good trade up there, in fact, incidents had been reported of muggings for passports in Yuzhno town on more than a few occasions. I had to stretch my legs, so I decided to have walk along the train. I reached the Buffet car there were a few drunks sat at the bar some young lads were messing about acting out a fight at the far end, the door opened two mean looking policemen dressed in black leather coats and the traditional Russian hats, machine guns over their shoulders, they stomped through casually pushing people out of their way, but the two young lads were not intimidated, they just ignored the two bully policemen. So the policeman pushed the two lads aside they resisted again, clearly giving lip back to their aggressors, the shorter of the two Policemen shouted and order to his colleague, who grabbed the two lads, in one motion the exit door was opened and the two boys were hurled from the train. I gasped in shock it was minus 30 out there, the snow was so deep walking will be hard going and of course there was no shelter for miles. I looked at the policemen they smiled shrugged their shoulders and closed the door then carried on their way like nothing had happened. My first thought was that those boys will freeze to death, looking pleadingly to the barman my face must have been a picture, he smiled shaking his head he picked up a phone, a minute later the train stopped to pick up the boys several minutes later the boys boarded the train, they were covered with snow and frozen, off they went to hug the pot belly stove. The two policemen appeared pointing at me and laughing I retreated to my cabin and locked the door with my cord.

Molikpaq, Sakhalin Island.

On board the rig "Molikpaq," more than half the crew were Russians and a mixture of tribes from "Papa New Guinea" and "East Timor" the rest of the crew were several expats. I met with the Casing crew from Papa New Guinea, in the locker room the next day, their Hydraulic unit had stopped. It was not my responsibility to fix their equipment the OIM explained to me that some of these guys were descendants from Cannibals, so of course I reluctantly agreed to look at their unit. I was introduced to the "Russian" chief Mechanic, "Oleg" a great fella he often offered to share his raw fish lunch with me but it was crap believe me my stomach hated me for a full week afterwards, You did not need directions to the toilets you just followed the smell the toilets were a much harder challenge than the food. I could not get on with the Russian food at all. It was so hard to get supply boats through the ice so, the rig had huge stores beneath the decks, it was like a Maze, The galley was a strange affair, it looked like any other Galley soon as I saw the food I knew I was gonna lose weight, the whole room and staff were ruled with a rod of iron by this huge woman, who towered over me and every other bloke in there she was a beast, no one dared criticize the food, when she saw me throw my food in the bin, she shouted something in Russian at me, I just nodded and walked out. At the rear of the Kitchen there was this really weird fella who spent all day sat on a wooden box peeling vegetables and chopping up fruit he looked like he was about to murder you, he made one feel really uncomfortable. I was warned not to speak to him apparently nobody ever spoke to him.

I asked my interpreter Valid,

"what's with that old fella over there I hear no one speaks to him,"

"if you speak to him Mike you better watch out because the last person who spoke to him got his jaw broken in 2 places he was once in the army bomb disposal unit in Afghanistan, he had some close calls he's never been the same since,"

The beast of a woman looked across at us in the corridor, she shouted at the old fella then just smiled at me then turned her back to him, the old fella threw his knife at her narrowly missing her by inches, it stuck in the serving hatch everyone stood waiting to be served took a dive for the floor. I looked the other way averting his glance.

The sunrise in this part of the world is stunning, one morning the entire horizon was bright pink, the icebreaker had left a trail of small icebergs around the rig which were only visible as they floated through a curtain of steam across the surface of the water (air is temperature gets so low the sea evaporates creating a curtain of steam raising from it) Boy did it look amazing, I ran up to the pushers office to get his digital camera wrestling my thermal work gear on I stumbled outside into the freezing air which took my breath away. I had to get a picture before the moment passed, I climbed up the rig wind wall to get an uninterrupted view hurriedly pulling out the camera from my heavy coveralls I pointed the camera at the stunning sunrise, I pressed the button nothing happened I cursed the bloody pusher for not renewing the batteries, a closer look revealed the digital display had frozen solid OPS! It was then I remember the warning Valid had told me,

"LCD displays freeze in these temperatures Mike so keep your mob phone display close to your skin!"

I ran up the decks to get the camera back in his desk, I ran back up to the office quickly stuffed the frozen camera in the drawer 30 seconds later the door opened,

"morning Mike how's it going, your early today"

"yes, I have got go for breakfast now,"

off I ran.

The next trip I found myself stuck in the Nogliki transit hotel no flights due to heavy snow and fog, the hotel was completely buried under the snow, access was just a tunnel big enough for one person to walk through, Alex the new interpreter was there as well, the sky was blue but damn it was so cold minus 48 degrees,

"Hey Mike, I will show you around the town,"

Alex said excitedly, he was so proud to be Russian.

"Are you kidding?" I said,

"it's too cold."

I was wearing long Johns and quilted coveralls, it was only 2 minutes before the chill started creeping up my legs, I knew he thought I was a British wimp. Alex was an Icon in these areas he was so handsome women swooned as he spoke to them, he pretended he didn't notice, he had the perfect physic to go with it, he made me sick!

"I will get a cab we will go into the village have some fun perhaps meet Eula she really likes you Mike, her baby loves the teddy bear you gave him for his birthday last trip."

Eula was the stewardess that cleaned my cabin she was a twin, her sister was the stunner she worked the rig laundry, half the rig crew casually hung around the rig laundry door just see her dancing around the room while she waited on the machines, she clearly loved the attention. Eula was not so slim a bit heavier around the face and waist, but she did have a great chest and she was great fun to be with she was a single parent. She struggled to make ends meet whenever I was leaving, I left her my loose change, on one occasion I had bought a teddy at the airport on my way through to the rig. I heard it was her son's birthday was imminent, so I gave it to her, Boy she was over the moon. Oil companies pay local labour very poorly whatever country their working in. My cabin was always spotlessly clean. Of course, rumours started about myself and Eula the other girls would tease me as they passed me in the corridor.

"Hey Mike, Eula, is for you I think," they laughed.

"Mike the Taxi is here come on it is very old as is Boris," Alex shouted,

 in front of me was a halftrack car! I'd never seen one before,

"amazing" I exclaimed.

A set of tracks in place of the rear wheels only on the movies had I seen this, the car itself looked like something from the fifties it was cosy and warm inside,

"it runs on gas Mike are you impressed?"

"You bet I am Alex."

 The smile on my face must have been ear to ear, I could not stop smiling the inside had a strong smell of well-aged leather. It covered all the seats, the front seat was a bench type the hand brake pulled out from under the well varnished wooden dash, the fascia was very basic it had two clocks, the Speedo and fuel gauge, wood adorned the edges of the doors picnic tables folded down in the back.

"This is Boris I take it,"

nodding to the person stood at the front of the car,

Alexi introduced Boris he turned to face me my first thought was hell how old is he his face was like a city road map the shiny row of gold teeth struck me dumb for a minute all his teeth were gold.

"Boris is 101, years old Mike, he has seen many cruel things in his life he speaks to no one. Rumour has it since he watched his family murdered by the communists, as they worked on the road of bones many years ago, Boris was also a sniper during the dispute with the Japanese over the south, he would lay in the snow waiting for hours then just shoot to injure the enemy so they would freeze to death. When the country he fought for murdered his family he just stopped talking he will write our fare down on a pad."

The car pulled smoothly away through the deep snow it was so bright glistening as it was sprayed into the sky behind the cars tracks, we passed a pair of black bears running away in to the forest, wolves could be seen lingering on the edge of the village it was a wonderful sight, I felt so privileged.

"Do the bears and wolves attack people Alexi?"

"Oh, you can never trust them Mike, we are all on the menu, you will see no one out walking without their shotguns."

"So where are all the shops and petrol stations."

Alexi laughed,

"this is not the UK, Mike, our shops are in these three-story blocks of flats,"

"how do you know which shops are in them."

"Mike there are few visitors here and large shop windows would crack in no time it is too cold."

Boris pulled over outside one of the grey blocks of flats Alexi paid and told Boris to come back in 2 hours. Once inside it was much warmer, sure enough there were shoe shops clothing shops and many more, including a bar there were maybe 6 people in it.

"Come Mike, we will drink vodka today it is Sakhalin's brand, maybe it will be too strong for you." laughed Alexi.

He was right, it was the fumes alone that took my breath away before it reached my lips, I am sure the other Russians noticed my struggling "right," I thought down in one, so down it went followed by me coughing my guts up. Alexi and Co laughed their heads off. I did manage another three before Eula the stewardess from the rig made an entrance, I knew her in passing as she entered the cabin and I left for work. She immediately saw what was going on, she sounded like she was having a row with Alexi.

"Mike I am sorry I thought it would be fun to get you drunk on good Russian Vodka."

He got real dirty look from Boris watching at the door, I could or most see myself in his bright gold teeth imagine polishing your teeth instead of cleaning them, I could just see him in the morning with his tin of Brasso rubbing his teeth in the mirror. Eula continued her heated exchange with Alexi, eventually he turned to me,

"Mike Eula wants to know if you would spend tonight with her at her house, no one will be flying tomorrow if there is a change, I will come for you," he smiled with a wink,

"Sounds great tell her it will be difficult as I speak no Russian,"

"she says it will not matter, she has cooked a stew and cleaned her house, since she had the Baby she has lived alone."

Eula smiled and took my hand "please come."

How could I possibly refuse, we got rousing applause as we left.

It was a 10-minute walk through the deep snow to her wooden house sat detached from the other houses it looked like it was round or a hexagon shape, it was hard to tell, smoke billowed out from her chimney. This was a set up by Alexi and Eula for sure, still I was up for a night with Eula she was always smiling, her ginger hair was long and bushy, it hung down past her large breasts, I could see by her tight jeans an hour glass figure. Her house was very clean inside as it would be as she cleaned the Rig cabins. Eula was talking in Russian she pointed to the window it was or most dark outside. It gets dark quite suddenly in this part of the world. We sat down to her hot stew it was not to my tasting but ok whatever it was. We drank some Vodka and drew pictures while we tried to communicate. It was late, Eula stood up and undressed I was surprised, she had a better figure than I thought large breasts, a narrow waist, good child baring hips, it was a good night.

I finally got to the Molikpaq rig the next morning, it was the day before Xmas eve so there was not a lot of work getting done, the guys were depressed that they were here for the Xmas period, others could not be bothered. The Platform called the Molikpaq was like a giant hexagon shaped tubular truncated pyramid rising up from the seabed. Then the whole column was filled with a million tons of sand, a semi sub rig was dropped on the top, basically that was it a very odd design, but it worked well the lowest access to the structure brought you down to the top of the column of sand, it was such a large expanse two large caterpillar bulldozers were required to keep the sand flat, and to get access to the stored containers, the crews often played football down there with room to spare, frequently crews went down there to settle arguments which turned rather violent sometimes with a bloody result. I once witnessed a fight which involved two lads armed with a hammer and a large length of wood both lads were flown to the hospital shortly after, but nothing more was said they never returned to the rig. I Spent most of my time in the machine shop since I was the only person on board who was qualified to use the lathes and milling machines, spares took a long time to arrive sometimes up to 6 months, it was largely due to the Rigs location and the weather, on one occasion I had to machine a locator adaptor jig to line up a transmission to the turbine generators, because the original had been damaged, the backup generator had stopped because the lads servicing it cross threaded the fuel filter housing, which meant there was no electricity on the rig. To copy the original jig was a complicated job, and time was against me the rig had to run on the much smaller 2nd emergency generator, which could only power the accommodation and essential services like fire pumps and the machine shop, there was no heating or lighting, the hydraulic systems had heaters as did the fuel systems otherwise they froze. By the time the tool was fitted the place was so cold the fuel and oil had started to freeze. Everyone on board had all their clothes on, it was so desperate my meals were brought to me in the machine shop, try operating a précis machine to limits of .005" with thick furry gloves on feet like blocks of ice and Alexi constantly muttering in my ear,

"Mike we are all depending on you the guys are all saying if this tool you are making does not fit, we will have to leave the platform and they will shut it down until spring and we will not be paid once we leave."

"Thank you Alexi no pressure then,"

"Mike the OIM and tool pusher are waiting on a progress report,"

"you must be kidding mate I can't stop to write a report tell them it will be quicker if they stop asking, it takes as long as it takes there are 7 separate diameters and 4 different recesses on this and they all need to be within .005," of their respective sizes and this lathe is at least 30 years old and come to think of it, if I screw this up there is only enough metal bar for one more tell them that."

This is normal for the oil industry if anything breaks down the drilling companies lose money hand over fist so as a mechanic, you're under tremendous pressure to get things running once more, plus of course all the computer work must be up to date. I once had a tool pusher come into my office,

"Mike why are you sitting here shouldn't you be outside checking stuff," I replied,

101

"John you should know by now if I am in here everything is ok, but if I am running around the deck then you should be worried because it means something is wrong."

He looked at me and frowned then walked out.

The tool was finished it was great and the bosses were pleased once the turbine generator was running once more, the Hydraulic tanks had frozen to slush so the oil was useless, so the next day we began the marathon task of changing the oil in every tank this was expensive one tank took 4×40 gallon barrels of oil there were several systems! The weather took a turn for the worst during the weeks that followed, the temperature fell to minus 32degrees so there was no flying which meant no crew changes for weeks, there were a lot of frustrated Russians looking for a fight.

There was one English TV channel on board "sky news" so some of us organised a (DVD) film show most nights so imagine yourself the only person from the west in the room, with twenty Russians, guess which film came on, the "Hunt for red October," in it the Americans make the Russians look stupid, I dared not leave in case I attracted attention to myself, I need not have worried the rig hard case Boris the roughneck shouted at me in Russian,

"what is he saying" I said quietly to Alexi,

"he wants to know why the Yanks make the Russians the underdogs in these films from the west,"

"Tell him I am not an American how the fuck should I know I am British the poor relation,"

Boris Laughed,

"Yes, you Brits are so poor, yet you think you are so special we have more history than you lot, but we don t live in it,"

Alexi laughed,

"he is correct Mike,"

I decided to shut up since he was right and besides I did not want to argue with him, I wonder at times how other Nations see us, I have had this said before I suppose it is true we do live in our history. The UK has not progressed at all since the war, Poverty and homelessness is a problem. The rich Government reap all the profits but don't invest in the Country.

At the end of my trip I had arrived in Nogliki with some other ex-pats the snow must have been ten feet deep, the drifts at the road sides were huge, wolves could be seen on the outskirts of the village clearly waiting for an easy kill, possibly a drunken Expat wondering away from the crowd. There was no train station but there was one shop near the railway line, so it doubled as a waiting room and community centre, The shop sold everything including the local manufactured booze (Vodka) which was going down a treat, after about ten minutes two ex-pats were out cold, I decided it wasn't for me I'm not good with booze. One of the prostrate ex pats was a guy I often worked with called Les he was lying outside in the freezing snow people here have died this way, so I pulled him inside the shop into the warm and out of reach of the wolves.

I was not able to bring him around, so I dragged him through the snow to the train, but the snow built up and created a drift in front of him making it slow going, the train was a good hundred yards away. I could see the train I was sure I saw some wolves on the far side, (these trains are high up to clear the snow). Luckily before I got there two official looking fellas stopped me and started talking in Russian, fortunately, Marina the company travel guide turned up.

"Mike if these policemen take him, he will end up in the local jail so he will miss his flight home, they want you to get him on the Train now or they will take him,"

"can't they see I am struggling, he's fucking heavy you know, and there's some wolves hanging around the train,"

Marina spoke to the policemen

"Mike they will not help you, but you have 10 minutes,"

I could see them turn their backs to me, they laughed,

"Hey, Mike, you need a hand,"

it was Oleg the Mechanic,

"you bet I need to get this drunken Brit on the train,"

Oleg called over his friends all clearly the worse for the Vodka, they hoisted Les up and on to the train, the top step must be twice my height, Oleg fired his gun into the air to scare off the wolves they are very big and made a blood-curdling growl, it made my skin crawl. Out in this wilderness, most people carry a gun not just for wolves but also the Bandits, and there are the muggers in Yuzhno, its survival of the fittest not just out there in Sakhalin, but also in Siberia, that's another story these places are too big and remote to police. Les slept the entire fourteen-hour trip to Yuzhno.

I managed several trips out to Sakhalin Island, but the travelling was getting me down, I was so tired once I got home, I was totally wiped out for a week it was a relief when I finished.

North Sea again.

My good buddy at Global (Debbie) got me more work filling in for Mechanics in the North Sea, I was on the Murchison overhauling the main engines assisting the Caterpillar Mechanics, we finished the job ahead of time without any incidents, everyone was impressed including me. I was so pleased with myself as I signed off my permit. I was brought out my daze,

"Hey, Mike can I have a word please," I looked around to see the source of the voice, in a rather large office sat an important looking person behind an even larger desk.

In the oil business the bigger the office the more intimidating you appeared to be, it's a bit like having a bigger dick than your mate.

"Come in Mike, please close the door"

He got straight to the point and asked me if I fancied more interesting work and better money. He appeared to be very self-assured, he looked important, this is my lucky day I thought opportunities like this have never come my way before, permanent employment had always eluded me for some reason, perhaps it was my wild side, always looking for adventure or a challenge.

"What sort of work is it?"

"Mechanic but mostly some inspection work,"

he said with a knowing smile

"I'll double your money how's that?"

"Sounds good to me yeah sure I'm in" "ok call me after this trip"

He handed me a card and muttered in my ear as he opened the door.

"Do you like working in foreign countries?"

"yeah," I eagerly replied,

Wow my path to big money had finally arrived I was due off home the next day, I could not wait to tell Karen she will be so pleased. I was so excited sleep eluded me that night, I was deep in thought of how I was going to spend all this cash. Once I was snugly strapped in to my seat on the chopper I was willing the flight to zoom by so I could zoom off home and tell Karen and the boys, I actually pulled a tendon in my neck trying to see the Shetland isles through the chopper window, which really annoyed the scaffolder sat next to me, he was sat next to the window in a strong Scottish accent he told me,

"Sit still man what's the matter with you,"

I could tell he was pissed off by the dagger looks he gave me,

"You have very piercing eyes" I told him laughing.

"Look land" I shouted,"

"I've landed a new job much more money,"

I told the irritated Scot, He just scoffed. The next part of your trip home from the North Sea, was a fixed wing to Aberdeen 45 minutes, once there I grabbed my bag and rushed off to my car. I sped all the way home excited new adventure's lay ahead into the unknown I go what a great job, something new every trip. Once home Karen had reservations at the thought of me going to foreign lands knowing my past.

"You are always getting involved into trouble of some kind, you need to settle,"

she knew I couldn't settle. A week later a call from Mark,

"Mike I want you to go to Abu Dhabi for me, I need you to survey the mud cleaning machinery on some land rigs and jack ups, you will need a camera and a laptop I will send you a template of the report to cut and paste from ok,"

"Err I don't have a laptop Mark, or a Digital camera,"

"No Problem Mike, go and buy them and claim it on expenses the job is for NDC, you will be met at the airport, I will send all the flight details and hotel arrangements to you, how does £400 a day sound."

"Brilliant," I eagerly replied,

"let me know when you are ready, I'll call you in the next five days."

I arrived in Abu Dhabi about a week or so after the Iraq's beheaded a British oil worker.

I had been out in the Desert for 3 weeks surveying mud systems on land rigs and Jack up Rigs. I had not seen another white man for weeks, there were no roads just orange sand in all directions as far as you could see, the odd drilling derrick could be seen on the horizon. All I had as a job description was list of rig numbers and their Mobil phone numbers. All I had to do was write a report on the condition of their mud systems and maintenance costs so that NDC could then see which machines were best to buy, their large fleet of 30 jack ups and 32 land rigs had a variety of different makes. I was living in the ADOC base camp a 4 hour drive into the desert from Abu Dhabi it was a very large camp about the size of a small airport one-half was workshops the other half was made up of double ended caravans, the galley was in the centre of the camp. I spent my spare time at the radio room located at the main gate, so I could see if any vehicle arrived from a rig on my list. I would find them on the camp and ask if I could come to survey the rig cleaning machinery. Often if certain operations were underway there would not be a vacant caravan for me to stay in overnight.

I found one particular thing on the camp fascinating; it was the wildlife; a natural pecking order had evolved. Dozens of cats roamed all over the camp along with chickens and their chicks, what I found amazing was the cats never hunted the chicks or hens, the hens supplied the camp with eggs and ate the bugs while the cats kept the rats and mice numbers down, all living in peaceful harmony of course to the Arabs this was all normal. Amid was the base manager he often invited me to his office for mint tea a real gent. There was a huge mint plant growing in the corner of his office it looked as if it was going to encompass the entire office, he was such a kind-hearted type he could not bring himself to trim it. Tea consisted of plain tea with two small (fingernail size) leaves from the plant floating in the tea, and very good it was too. The offices were very busy, stewards dressed in black trousers white shirt pink tie and gold waistcoats, finished off by mega shiny black shoes very smart, funny thing though none of them were over five foot in height. They swiftly darted silently around from office to office with tea or documents very civilised, in fact, more so than any office block I experienced in the UK, in fact, all the staff were very polite.

Every morning I worked my way through the phone list of land rigs hoping they would let me visit and stay overnight quite often there was no spare caravan. It was going rather well I was well through my list there was just 3 rigs left, until rig 25 came up. It was an 8-hour drive through the sand dunes, it was the oldest rig in the NDC (National drilling company) fleet, I had been warned by the Manager of a previous rig I visited,

106

" you will not be happy on rig 25 Mike it is very old and very dirty the Rig manager is an idiot he does not look after his men he is an Egyptian they think they are the superior Arab, he and I are not friends, Mike tell him I say his father was a camel,"
I had to laugh but he really meant it,
I was at rig 9, work started very early because the heat at midday was unbearable at 40 degrees, by 11 am I was rushing for shelter, I got a bit involved one day I was anxious to finish the rig it was just as the previous rig manager had told me, the heat caught me out, I was suddenly feeling quite sick and weak my legs felt like jelly, it suddenly washed over me like a rush of wind, I reached for my bottle of water, I always carried one, to my horror it was empty. It was a fair distance back to the shelter of the offices without the chance of shelter from the intense heat, walking through the fine sand is hard going it's a bit like walking in deep snow, your feet sink into the sand covering your feet completely, it's a bit like dragging a heavy weight behind you sapping all the strength from you in minutes, no wonder people die out here.

If you've ever had a woman sink her nails into your back then drag them down your back, that is how the sun feels as it burns into your skin the instant you step out of the shade, in my case my bald head. Stupidly I had left my hard hat in the permit office, it was also too far away to go back. I set off holding my small backpack over my head but only in a short distance found my strength draining away fast, my arms were soon too tired to support the backpack, I lowered it forward over my eyes to serve as a sun shade, I tried to throw up but nothing was forthcoming just a sore throat. It was crazy! I could see the camp in the distance and yet it might as well have been miles away. considering my situation, it dawned on me I may not make it! It makes one realise how very delicate and fragile the human body is and the very narrow window of conditions we survive in.

My knees felt weak and shaky I dropped to my knees strangely one thought in my mind,

"these Arabs are gonna think I am one stupid white man but then anyone would think that watching me."

Saved! I hear an engine approaching from behind.

"Thank fuck"

It was Billy? (An Arab called Billy??) The rig driver

"Mike you ok? You should not be out in the sun you could die especially as you are a white man, we Arabs are much tougher than you guys."

laughed Billy as he helped me to my feet.

Once in the safety of the office and refreshed with a bottle of warm water, nausea had left me. Apparently, it is not good practice to drink chilled water after an experience like I'd had.

"Come my friend we will eat then you will feel better"

Billy stood there with a tray of sandwiches a big grin running over his face,

"are you serious Billy"

"of course, Mike please eat Mina at head office will be really unhappy if he has to report that you are dead, and the sheik will be very angry with him."

Amir the rig manager chuckled at Billy, so I tried a bite, or two Billy handed me a cup of mint tea. They were such good people out of all the 13 land rigs and 8 jack-up rigs I inspected there were only two maybe 3 people that gave me bad vibes a better average than the North Sea.

This had really surprised me, before my trip out there I had the Arabs figured as hard and ruthless mainly through the bad press in the UK. How wrong I was to make a judgement by reputation these are good caring people who watch out for each other, what an injustice when an entire population form an opinion of a culture from the press alone yet be so wrong. I was a white man alone and the treatment I received from the Arabs was so good I felt humbled and embarrassed at myself and my fellow Brits at our arrogance for considering our culture as benchmark.

Billy dropped me off at the rig 25 managers caravan but declined to come in with me I let myself in the office, I removed my boots which was the rule out there I was met by the medic who doubled up as safety officer a very well-spoken Indian,

"call me Pasha,"

"I'm Mike pleased to meet you,"

After the very boring Induction video this is mandatory before venturing on to the rig, it is so you are aware of what's going on and what to do if there is a blowout or a fire. Then I met the Egyptian manager.

"You can call me Mr Ebo, I believe you are known as Mr Mike,"

his arrogant tone pissed me off.

I told him firmly,

"I am here to do an inspection so I may need co-operation from the electrician and Mechanic,"

the word inspection was met with raised eyebrows.

"What sort of inspection?"

he demanded,

I told him it was just a mud handling survey, he brightened up considerably. To lighten the mood

I laughed,

"bet you thought I was here to check up on you eh."

He frowned looked very serious for a few seconds which worried me at first then he cracked a smile and said,

"you English always trying to be funny sometimes it is good to be funny but not all Arabs see the funny side, so be careful who you speak to Mike there are a few Palestinians, here they are very sensitive and always looking for trouble so see you later."

He eyed the door,

Pasha showed me to my caravan it was like all the caravans it was very old the first thing I noticed was the huge sand dune up against the side, as we got closer I could see it was no dune, the caravan was tilted at a steep angle, if that was not bad enough as I pushed open the rusty door, I had to step over a large hole in the centre of the floor.

"The air conditioner is broken Mike it will be very hot here tonight,"

Pasha said cautiously, as if he was expecting a heated reply,

"I bet it doesn't bother these flies eh I be better sleeping outside,"

109

I barked at him,

"Oh yes Mike I have fly spray for you the manager he said you would need it,"

"You must be having a laugh Mate why is this place such a mess,"

I was pissed off.

I could not stay in this shit hole, but I didn't have a choice, I did get some sleep, but I ended up with a sore throat from overuse of the fly spray. Amid was right this guy was a bastard he clearly fixed this for sure, I made up my mind the report I write will condemn his rig in fact Ill speak with Mina at the head office soon as I get back to Abu Dhabi. The rest of the rig was as bad as my accommodation was.

The survey was going fine I found nothing good about the rig machinery or mud systems it had been neglected. I got invited into the electrician's office (a caravan) great I thought it was so hot outside in 48 degrees of heat, air conditioning boy was that welcome, as I entered and squeezed past the desks, I caught site of the TV Tucked away in the corner showing the video of the oil worker being beheaded with a small pen knife, the audience of several Arabs found it funny, I could tell by the laughing which scared the hell out of me.

"Mr. Mike Please come over sit Please,"

the electrician ushered me to the chair at his desk.

The first thing I noticed about this man was his snake eyes, in fact, he looked like a snake, you can't trust a snake, I thought then it came to me, lee van clef in the film good bad and the ugly he looked like a Pakistani version.

"Mike! how are you liking our rig it is very good yes the manager is good to us,"

he said smiling,

"are you taking the piss mate it the worst rig I v seen so far,"

"You're a very funny man Mike,"

"I am not being funny pal, is your maintenance up to date, can I see the PM system,"

I knew it would not be few maintenance crews ever managed it.

The creepy smile slowly disappeared from his

face and the eyes narrowed,

"mm" I thought

"touched a nerve I think"

"are you here to inspect us?" he asked

"Oh yes of course."

110

He looked even more worried now but not as much me I had suddenly become aware of the TV audience who were clapping I sneaked a look over to see that they were clapping at coronation street in Arabic and these guys seemed to think it was hilarious. I found it a very boring program.

The electrician decided to try and lighten the atmosphere sensing my displeasure,

"Alfred is my name,"

Smiling, I said

"a Pakistani called Alfred that's really weird so your good friends with the rig manager are you Alfred,"

I chuckled.

"Oh yes we all love him he is a great man he looks after us,"

Alfred excitedly blurted.

I quizzed him further,

"this place is a mess, how can you think that Alfred you are an educated man he has a bad reputation with the other rig managers, as arrogant and a snob this rig needs a hell of a lot of money spending on it, if Mina at head office saw it he would be really angry.

Alfred interrupted,

"Mike this is why you should not be here we believe he has secrets, I'm sure, but we do not question him he gives us a bonus every month but we cannot talk about it so please, Mike make a good report for us but you must be leaving very soon he has two large roughnecks who protect him, if he hears you are making a bad report he will be very angry."

My situation had suddenly become serious why does he give the crew a monthly bonus? And why does he have a couple of heavies. I was worried, what lengths would Mr Ebo go to silence me. It is a long drive across the desert to the nearest road if you knew which direction to go. It would be easy to make a body disappear out here and no one would know for a long-time. Perhaps I was getting carried away, I had to lighten the mood, so I said,

"got you going there eh Alfred"

laughing he replied,

"Very funny Mike but it is you who will be sleeping in the black hole tonight"!

"What the hell is the black hole"?

"The caravan you slept in last night but if you finish work today you won't have to,"
he laughed!
"Good idea I could try and finish today, I'll call Billy to come and pick me up."
"good idea Mr Mike call him now,"
Alfred was nervous,
I stepped outside and called Billy, I slipped down the narrow gap between the caravans so no one could hear me, I was in a hurry to leave now my imagination was running wild.
I waited an eternity for Billy to answer the phone, I could see Alfred stepping into the manager's office now I was scared!
"Hello, Mike" it was Billy,
"hi buddy I need you to come quick, I think I'm in a bit of trouble here,"
"ok Mike I'll be about 2 hours."
"Shit, Billy, I know something is going on and I think Ebo knows I know, he may even prevent me from leaving, I'll need a distraction so I can sneak off."
"I'll be over at the water well, it's about half a mile away from the rig."
"I know it, Mike you sound scared Mike, maybe I'll hurry."
"you think I'm shitting it right now Billy, but I have an idea."
It meant walking in the 46 degrees of heat for the half mile, just like a few days ago but this time, I have my hat and a bottle of water, I discreetly made my way through the cluster of containers and trailers to the high voltage control container, I removed the plastic handle from the main breaker then I tripped it, I chucked the handle down the back of the switchgear, the rig would now be without power so Alfred and the crew would be busy sorting it, I crept away without being seen. It was hard going I followed the water pipeline but there were so many dunes to traverse and with my feet sinking into the sand it was making it very hard going progress was slow, the heat was draining me faster than I thought it would, the sweat was running into my eyes. As I crested the next dune, I saw a tanker truck there were two men moving around it, as I approached, they looked up smiling,
"White man what the hell are you doing out here are you lost or just crazy?"

112

I leaned against the truck to get my breath and shelter from the sun my skin was burning like hell, I turned to check the position of the pipe, I was stunned there was two gun barrels poking out from the driver's seat I nearly shit myself.

"I could ask you the same mate," I said as calmly as I could.

"Don't you see white man we're working please leave us," Arab one replied,

I noticed a hose connected to a well head through a hole in the wire fence, I realised what was going on, I nearly shit myself I knew I had to show ignorance and hope these two didn't realise I had clocked them or they'll likely shot me. I had to be confident.

"Do the lads at the rig know you've arrived, Alfred never mentioned you had turned up shall I call him"? I got my phone out, to my great relief they never flinched.

"Please tell him we have money to pay Mr. Ebo,"

"the manager ah yes I'm not permitted that honour,"

"I call him Mr. Manager,"

I stepped aside to pretend to make the call,

"He says to pay me now," I joked,

they babbled away in Arabic then the one that spoke English just told me to fuck off. So, I carried on following the freshwater pipeline, I just hoped Billy would arrive before the rig manager or Alfred realised what was going on. It crossed my mind that he could be selling the oil illegally. Then it dawned on me I was getting drawn into this and way over my head. I could see the pump house not far now; I was feeling rather ill and weak. I was praying Billy would be there waiting for me I normally don t scare easily, but on this occasion, I could feel it creeping over me. I v been in a lot of sticky situations in my time abroad, but I was so isolated out here it would be easy to make a person vanish, it would be a long time before the alarm was raised and by that time the body would be or most impossible to locate. I tried to call the office, but my credit had all but run out maybe I had enough to call Billy once more, I decided to save it hell I only came to do an inspection of the mud cleaning machinery, now it was growing arms and legs never mind the fucking inspection, Reaching the pump house by the skin of my teeth was a great relief, shade from the sun at last and water in good supply downing a pint or two just made me feel nauseous, like an amateur I had drunk too much too fast. I sat down by the pump in the hut the insects and a couple of scorpions scurried away as I slumped down in the shade, I was too exhausted to care or to expect the jeep to arrive at any moment after what seemed like an age I started to worry perhaps Billy was part of it perhaps he was at the rig with Alfred deciding what to do with me. No, I decided my imagination was running wild Billy will arrive and take me back to the base camp.

"Mr. Mike please wake up we must hurry,"

It was Billy shaking me I had fallen asleep the heat had got the better of me I threw up a couple of times then crawled into the jeep it was so cool; I immediately felt a bit better.

"It took me hours to get here, Mike, will you be ok,"

Billy handed me a bottle of water,

"drink slow Mike stick your head out the window if you feel sick or you will be cleaning up the mess," Billy laughed.

Water well pump house.

It was not long before I felt I could talk without throwing up, of course, it does not help driving over sand dunes that alone makes you feel seasick.

"Billy, there were 2 guys pumping oil from the well into a tanker and I am sure it can't be legal,"

I blurted out rather hurriedly Billy just laughed.

"Mike to fast my English is not that good,"

"I had a chat with the rig Manager Mr. Ebo and Alfred the electrician it turns out these guys get unofficial bonus payments, no questions asked, Mr. Ebo seemed very uncomfortable about me doing my inspection also Pasha warned me to be careful who I spoke to, so I decided I better leave because if I produce a bad report the rig will undergo an enquiry which Mr. Ebo does not want the only thing to do would be to stop me carrying out the report."

I told Billy about the two guys at the tanker and how they were going to pay Mr. Ebo.

"We will talk to Amid Mike but for now you should sleep you will feel better and your face is very badly burnt"

I looked in the mirror to see my face was so red and blistered then for some reason it started to hurt like hell.

"Shit I wish I was at home,"

"What was that Mr Mike?"

"oh, nothing Billy just me dreaming,"

what a mess I'm in, my face covered with blisters. I had some pain killers in my backpack I nodded off to sleep within minutes.

I woke up as we drove into the base camp.

"Dam Mike what the hell have you been up to, the rig manager from 25 told me you had disappeared in the desert looks like he was right I'll get the nurse to look at you, your face is a mess."

Amid was very concerned it seemed, I sat down the busy little waiter dressed so smartly in the white shirt and gold waistcoat brought me a cup of mint tea, it was the remedy for most ailments out here although it is soothing. I listened to Billy repeating my story to Amid, as I drank, I noticed the blisters on the backs of my arms and hands which did sting, I dreaded the nurse's attention it's gonna hurt I'm sure,

"Mike we will talk later you must see the nurse your burns are very bad you should know better than wondering out in the heat it will make you hallucinate and it seems you have done according to Billy he says he found you asleep in the pump house."

Billy took me to my caravan I was still weak; I am sure I had sun stroke the nausea was still present I lay down on the bed to wait for the nurse."

"I will come for you later Mike" Billy said as he left.

At this point my face and arms felt as if they were on fire the nurse came in a few minutes later she was an Indian woman about 30 years old slim petite and well spoken

"Oh, dear these burns are bad Michael you will have to protect yourself when you leave this trailer, I will treat you, but you must stay in here for a few days I will have food sent to you."

The lotion stung like hell I was tempted to take it off her and chuck it away, she laughed as she easily avoided my pathetic attempt at grabbing the bottle from her,

"don't be silly Michael your blisters will burst I am the nurse please do as I say and lie still."

"what is your name, or do I just call you nurse,"

"No, I am a doctor if you make advance to me Michael you will be in serious trouble the men here are very possessive of their women."

"I am happily married" I assured her.

"Arab men do not approve of Moslem women with western men." she left as quietly as she arrived.

My next thought was to call home but I remembered I had used up most of my credit I had left my UK contract phone at the hotel because it had a camera, which I was told are not allowed out here in the oil fields what nonsense, my thoughts took me back to my first trip out here, I got a pay as you go phone in Abu Dhabi They are very strict out here, in fact, two Americans on the same transport as me had theirs taken from them and to their horror watched as the phones were smashed on the roadside while we were at the checkpoint. The two of them were then quick marched straight back on the transport at gun point all comments completely ignored by the mean-looking soldiers.

"Don't want to mess with these guys"

I warned the two yanks as they boarded the transport who were clearly disturbed and shocked at their treatment at the hands of the soldiers. The Doctor had left the door open possibly to let the breeze flow through the trailer to cool it for me, a cat chasing a rodent brought me out of my daydream as it scurried across the slippery floor. My eyes stung as they opened quickly cursing the cat for scaring me, I sat up to see the Doctor watching me.

"You seem ok Michael, you have been asleep for a long time how do you feel?"

I got up walked over to mirror dam my face is a mess, I looked terrible "lotion will soon heal it Mike, don t worry a week or two and you will never know it happened."

I walked over to see Amid I asked him to call Mina in Abu Dhabi,

"I have already run your story past him he told me to get you back asap there's transport leaving in 2 hours get something to eat and pack I 'll see you at the gate."

What a relief but I was still worried Mr. Ebo could still reach me or have someone come after me, Amid left the office so I grabbed his phone, I dialled the office in Aberdeen Mark answered.

"Hey, Mike I hear your having fun and games out there will you go out to the jack-ups after your finished,"

I interrupted,

"Mark shut up and listen I need to tell you something I quickly ran through my little episode

"Mike the sun has got to you I heard you collapsed from heat exhaustion how's your burnt face coming on?"

"No, it all happened, before that Mark there is something illegal going on just like I told you, I actually meet the tanker drivers who were filling their tanker. As I spoke to them, they had their money ready to pay the manager Mr. Ebo and the Rig electrician.

"How far have you got with the reports,"

"This was the last one because it was so far away, I left it to last."

"Ok then get back to town stay in a good hotel have a few days off then see how you feel we can discuss the illegal goings on I'll speak to Achmed and arrange it all" He hung up. I heard a noise behind me I spun around it was the little waiter with my mint tea he placed it on the desk he whispered close my ear,

"Mr. Ebo is a bad man."

"Then he was gone as silent as a ghost he vanished clearly, he feared something Amid arrived and sat down behind his desk,

"enjoy your tea Mike,"

"yes of course, so is there any feedback from my little escapade?"

"yes 2 fighter jets and a helicopter are out there, the two Terrorists were captured but refused to acknowledge that Mr Ebo or Alfred were involved."

"They are lying, like I said they did offer money for Mr Ebo and refused to use me as a go between."

A thought suddenly occurred to me perhaps this is deeper than I first thought perhaps they're all involved in this how far does it go as far as Mina! Perhaps or that snake, Baasin the go between back in town, he was Marks contact at the Abu Dhabi agency. I never did trust him, What the fuck am I doing, am I going mad, I was starting to doubt myself did it ever happened. Billy! I wonder if he is involved, I got up to leave the office.

"Mike I will arrange your hotel in Abu Dhabi, please do not worry about anything go to town have fun, I will give you my card for the 69 club you will like it live band and mostly women are there I will tell the manager you will be there, he will give you free drink and women."

Billy was sat in his jeep outside the office block.

"Mike I will run you to your caravan come get in,"

"No, it's ok Billy, I'll walk it's not far,"

"you are to stay out of the sun Mike, Doctor told you, so please get in or she will beat me,"

I laughed, "you are scared of a woman Billy I thought you guys were dominant in the Muslim religion, and women were 2nd class?"

"Oh yes in the Koran it is written but in true life Mike we men are puppets for women to play with just as it is for you white men."

Billy chuckled,

"come Mike I will get you some food we walked over to the galley the chickens and their chicks scattering as we passed, once in the cool of the galley I was centre of attention since I was the only white man in the camp, and of course my episode out in the desert was quickly becoming common knowledge. I could see the fingers pointing at my very burnt face, it still hurt of course, once sat down with my meal which I must say was very good, also the table manners of the Arabs is better than I've seen on some of the UK Rigs. I caught the eye of an old Indian man dressed in a white gown, he was a huge man easily 6'6" he clearly commanded respect from everyone, he wore a round wide brimmed white hat, he came and sat down with us he glanced at Billy who nodded, Billy smiled and moved to another table.

"Hey Billy, what you are doing" I said,

"it's ok Mike" he smiled nodding at the old fella. The man in white smiled and said in a quiet tone,

"I am the cleric or preacher in your language my son is the only Muslim cleric to convert to Christianity, but I forgave him but he was murdered after he wrote his book called "In search of you" his name "Maulvi Sulaimon".(look it up).

"I am not here to convert you, Mike, I can see you are a good person, I must warn you not to get involved in any troubles out here, it is a disease creeping through our people, I studied at your University of Cambridge many of the students are charlatans without sympathy they think they are above us mortals such arrogance I found it sickening so I came back."

The smile was replaced with an angry frown, it is greed Mike, it takes over men once they have money, they want more do you have money Mike?" his intense stare was intimidating.

"Err No I don t," I muttered.

He lowered his eyes level with mine and firmly said.

118

"Go home Mike we can sort out our own problems you would just be hurt, there are many insurgents out here and some are on rig 25.

He stood up looked around the room and left without a word. I looked down at the table he had left the book right under my nose, (I still Have to this day).

Billy hurriedly returned excitedly he enquired,

"ok Mike tell me everything he said, he has never talked to someone privately like that, what did he say to you? did he tell you to leave he is the important man here the rebels have tried twice to kill him."

"Here on the camp" I exclaimed,

"oh yes Mike, many Arabs pass through the camp you cannot patrol the entire desert this camp is like an oasis, so as they pass here they are monitored by hidden cameras around the fences, and that is why there is only one gate, I hear that the UK has more cameras watching the people than any other country, Mike how can you call your country a free society?"

"I personally don't Billy, it is a bad place the rich persecute the less fortunate it is an illusion,"

As we walked to my caravan in silence, I wondered why I still called it home, it is in fact anything but a free Country.

Billy smiled smugly; I had no answer for him he was right of course I closed the door of my caravan, I laid down to ponder my little adventure.

(There is more freedom out here in the wilderness, just Mother Nature making the rules you cross her at your peril. The more I think about it the more I believe that the bubble of civilisation will one day burst, and Mother Nature will wipe out the virus that is infecting her domain! Mankind the only one of Mother Nature's creations that takes what it wants from the planet but unwilling to adapt to an evolving environment i.e. planet Earth instead he tries to change the environment to suit himself selfishly ignoring the consequences on the rest of nature. She will take restitution).

Terrorists here in Abu Dhabi that's a scary thought I suppose if they are in the UK which we all know they are there because Tony Blair's government let them in so why not out here, I had crossed their sort once before in Nigeria which scared the hell out me, These people believe so passionately in their cause you cannot negotiate with them they do not know the meaning of mercy, pity or compassion, one can only respect their total commitment, what's even more scary is the fact that no one has ever conquered them. Any one of these guys on this camp could be a terrorist. Hell, I got to get out of here, who knows the selling of the oil illegally could be funding their operations. I better go home before it's too late. I awoke suddenly to a banging on the door it was Billy.

"Mike you must come I have your lift to Abu Dhabi"

Opening the door stood there was a young man in his early twenties he was immaculately dressed in the traditional Dish Dash.

"ok I'm all packed and ready to go mate."

He walked in like he owned the place,

"I will not be carrying your bags for you like the other Arabs I am not like them as you will see"

He spoke in a stuck-up sort of manner as the snobs do at home, he looked me up and down smiled,

"Come please I will be driving; you may sit up front with me if you wish"

I felt like a child getting an order from Dad, I had to smile the last thing I wanted was to upset this man after all he is my ticket back to the airport and away from here.

"Call me Hazmat Mike what is your family name"?

"Youngman what's yours"

"That is your name truly, it is a strange name Mike you are clearly not that young,"

he laughed as he slammed the jeep door.

Hazmat

I settled into the plush seat this was evidently the very best of jeeps I was ready for the 5-hour drive. An hour past without conversation such was the standard of this vehicle I did not get the feeling of sea sickness I normally did while traversing sand dunes. I felt I had to say something and I was about to but something appeared in the distance, it was some sort of settlement, as we got closer it turned out to be what I would call a camel ranch. We pulled up to the fence several camels came up to the fence, I looked around to see who would greet us but there was no one there.

"Youngman this is where we breed the racing camels, they are not friendly so be careful,"

He walked through a small gate into the compound and stroked one, "come Mike it will be ok,"

"I don t think so Mate these buggers look evil and they stink too"

I could hear the camels growling Hazmat made a quick retreat he was clearly showing off.

Hazmat Posing.

Sometime later we reached a real road we had been driving for 3 hours, we saw only 2 other cars, I must have drunk 3 litres of water I needed a pee. I told Hazmat he indicated we will be stopping soon and sure enough to my great amazement as we turned off the road drove around a great sand dune there was a huge building to my astonishment a fucking car museum why out here of all places. I could not think of any possible reason why one would build one here so far out the way.

The Museum

"Hazmat"

I held up my hands towards the building shrugging my shoulders he laughed.

"Come,"

We got out of the jeep we walked toward the door the car park was empty not a single person for possibly 100 miles or buildings it was completely isolated! The building was just like a Castle wall there was one small glass door at the front no windows at all. At the front was the vehicle used in the first star wars movie the one used by the sand people bit like a tracked box really, Hazmat pulled out a set of keys from his pocket and unlocked the door. That's it I thought he must be from an important family he acted like he owned the place he reached into a fridge near the entrance and handed me an ice cream. We walked through the dark hallway Hazmat open a switch box and switched on the lights which were quite dim, he was clearly happy to be here.

"come Mike see my cars are they beautiful yes,"

the lighting was not very bright but I could see there must have been a few hundred cars a lot of them were from films like Vanishing point, Herbie the beetle, a whole range of old Mercedes from the early 1940s Ferraris Matisse Rolls Royce jaguar, it was an extensive collection to many to list, we walked around for an hour or so not anther soul to be seen, I can only presume it was a private collection as we left Hazmat answered a call.

"Are we leaving,"

I beckoned to him he held up a hand

"moment please,"

I had feeling something was a foot my phone rang, it was Mina,

"Mike how are you my friend where are you,"

I told him,

"that is good Mike we have a favour to ask you, please could you commission a rig for us it is not far from your position it is a rig we have built using our spares from the yard, I have spoken to Mark your boss he is fine he tells me it should only take you a couple of days, I know this is a surprise but you will be rewarded, ADOC the client is sure that the rig will not pass the inspections and the client's representative will be there, Mike do not take shit from him he will be very critical and difficult."

"Ok Amid I will go did you check out my story about the rig 25 manager?"

Mina assured me,

"Please, Mike, forget, we will check it out."

I'm sure I could hear a faint chuckle in the background as he hung up. I looked around for Hazmat, I spotted him talking to some other guys who had turned up all wearing dark glasses and chequered tea towel's around the head and neck least that's how it looked to me. I decided not to take anything to seriously anymore, this was all a game to them. I decided I would do this job then go home; the heat was getting quite oppressive now I actually missed the constant rain we get in the UK. I could tell these lot were talking about me, so I casually walked up to the four of them all well-dressed clearly none of them has ever seen a hard day's work in their lives. I received the usual gold teeth smile and handshake fingers adorned with gold rings their hands were soft and weak, I was right this lot lived a blessed life,

"ok what's the plan Stan anyone speak English" I asked,

The sheik smiled,

"oh yes Mike, please come in my jeep we will go to the rig it is maybe an hour from here."

We set off in convoy of 4 Posh Toyota land cruisers speeding across the sand I was sick of orange sand it's all you can see nothing else just sand. I actually hated leaving the tarmac road because the sand dunes made me feel seasick.

"Mike none of us know anything about machines we just invest money do you invest Mike?"

I laughed. "no, I have no money what's your name sir?" I asked him

"just call me Sheik Zayed!"

An hour or so later I spotted a drilling derrick on the horizon, worse still there was a lot of sand dunes between us and the rig. I grabbed a bottle of water hopefully to take my mind off nausea. We reached rig without me throwing up. It all looked like new, the testing went ok but one problem, the ADOC rep decided one mud trough was not right because there was a 12" pipe passing through it, thus decreasing the capacity, so I had a welder change it overnight, from then it was like clockwork at four pm the following day it was completed and everyone was pleased me included, now I can go home I had been in the desert for 2 months and my face still stung like hell, I mused thank fuck real food rain and most of all sex, the strongest instinct a man has it raises itself to the fore front of your mind, the longer you've been without it the stronger it is, it seemed an age away right now.

"Mike today no work we will have a party, come I will show you." the Sheik, proudly announced.

Sheik Zayed walk me towards a large dune and announced with his smiling gold teeth.

We walked over the large sand dune, once at the top the site that met me was quite extraordinary. It was like a scene from a film, a huge marquee had been erected a small diesel driven air con unit parked by it, a long matt had been laid out leading to the entrance and there were the dinky little waiters from the base camp in their gold waistcoats and pink ties swiftly waiting on some tables under an umbrella at the entrance, and sat there was Abdul and his pals with Hazmat.

"who is Hazmat Abdul he must be from a privileged family is he"?
Abdul smiled

"he is the son of a sheik, but I cannot tell you who, come on Mike, we must go in, the speeches will start soon."

As usual a minute after the speeches started, I was nodding off, after all it was all in Arabic, Until I was summoned up to the

Lector Abdul had to nudge me awake.

"Mike you must go up to the Sheik,"

I jumped up I had missed the bit about me, so I just walked up to the sheik he was smiling revealing a row of gold teeth he handed me a black box,

"Mike please enjoy this small gift as our appreciation of your patience with us,"

I thanked them for their generosity and what a pleasure it has been for me to work with such distinguished people, I returned to my seat.

The order to eat was given so all the sheiks and their minders scurried off to fight for the freshest prawns.

The box contained a black metal Nokia 8800 Sirocco mobile phone which at that time cost £1000.00 it had all the extras, blue tooth extra batteries, stand all very high-quality stuff I was chuffed to bits.

All the rig crews were stuffing themselves the food was quite amazing fresh lobster, crab prawns salad alcohol-free beer, all chilled and fresh and right out here 5 hours' drive from the nearest town. I was impressed it's amazing what can be done when money is no object.

Once Back in Abu Dhabi Abdul dropped me off at the Royal meridian hotel.

"Mike, please stay here long as you like it is all paid for just tell your boss to arrange your flight when you need it, make sure he gets you a first class seat if not you must tell me."

He handed me his card, white, embossed with gold leaf print adorned across the business card. This is Xmas I thought.

"Yes, sir thank you very much, Abdul, I am so happy,"

"anything you need Mike call me."

He drove off into the crazy rush of traffic the concierge for hotel grabbed my bags,

"please sir come this way,"

This place is a palace was my first thought as I looked up at the huge building in front of me, huge hallways all marble it was cool Inside this was so great the only time I'd seen quality like this was on Bond movies. The women on the desk were all perfect, immaculately presented beautifully dressed they were untouchable and so polite and spoke perfect English.

"Mike Youngman, we have a special booking for you, it is by order of the Sheik so you will have our best room and you can use all the facilities there is no charge."

I felt so underdressed for this place I must have looked a right mess stinking too everyone else wore suits and thawb.

"Sorry for my appearance I v been out in the desert for a few weeks."

"Mr. Mike perhaps I am cheeky, but you are a hero we are told."

she said smiling, I was stunned at the same time confused I laughed,

"no, I am not why would you think that."

"You are the English man who helped the sheik during his negotiations with some terrorists, it is said you uncovered the plot by the terrorists to steal our oil."

I was stunned a smile forced its way to my mouth, I thought for a moment it all fell into place.

"boy news travels fast out here"

I replied laughing.

Once up my enormous room I sat in the huge bath for a while contemplating the events in the past week, those guys at the tanker were the terrorists.

shit why did they not shoot me maybe they could not afford to attract any attention so they played along, fucking hell no one will believe this at home, best not mention it I suppose, I pondered it for a while I will stay here a few days then go home I informed Mark.

Debbie from the agency emailed me she knew what had happened, I called her, she excitedly started

"Mike you are all over the oil companies data site no one would believe me when I told them it was you, are you ok?"

"I'm ok my face was badly burnt but I'm ok bit worried that the terrorists might try shoot me so I'm staying in, this is a fantastic hotel so I'm not leaving, the Sheik has it all paid for lol."

"Mike" Debbie sounded excited, "will you come to see me when you arrive back in Aberdeen, I have a new house and a new car perhaps I could show you."

"ok Debbie Ill be in touch soon."

Nigeria.

Four months later, after my meeting with Debbie and a few trips offshore for her. I get a call from Mark,

"Mike how do you feel about going to Nigeria for a couple of weeks you will be with an electrician, Bill Brown, I have everything organised flights the accommodation, you will be staying in the Shell secure compound. You will have 8 soldiers with you when travelling organized by a good contact, his name is Colonel Omni, any problems you call him, I'll email you all the contacts and flight arrangements I will pay you £700 a day all you have to do is survey the condition of two land rigs and two swamp barges, then make a report."

"no problem when I leave,"

"couple days,"

"ok Thanks Mark this will be a great change from the North Sea I didn't t want to go back there it had become boring and so monotonous."

Preventative Maintenance systems had been adopted to try and cut "down time" which meant maintenance was just routine checks prescribed by some computer in town, it was so routine you even had the same checks every trip.

Once I put the phone down, I remembered the last trip to Nigeria at least, this time, I'll have 8 soldiers with me, I tried to assure myself, then the memories came flooding back, I had been terrified had. Had I made a mistake returning there, I was a man of my word I had never let anyone down the entire time I had worked in this industry, plus of course once you start to turn work away the phone calls start to go away too. I met Bill the electrician at Charles De Gaulle airport he was an old school type like me, but taller well-built long dark hair good looking bloke quite a cool type, so that was good but not a talkative type he sat next to me at the gate and said nothing for an hour. He later told me he had recently lost his wife to cancer,

"so sad I am sorry Bill."

It had left him, and his young daughter devastated hard to imagine the grief that consumed him. (Unfortunately, I did later in my life.) So once again I found myself asking that same old question.

"Is there a god?"

My answer for myself is No, there is not, but if I am wrong, he must be a right cruel God the amount of suffering that he allows us to endure is contrary to everything he preaches in the Bible!

"Talk is cheap."

Religion is a hard and cruel concept to have faith in, yet people do, God said he created us in his image, when considering the state of the planet and how utterly cruel we can be to each other that really doesn't reflect well on him does it!

Port-Harcourt airport is a small domestic airport with little or no system of immigration, local baggage snatchers were still preying on the unknowing arrivals by grabbing their luggage from them carrying it to the transport then demanding payment. So little had changed since my first visit. I, of course, remembered this little game I had a tug of war with this young lad over my two bags, we reached the bus still determinedly he held on I shouldered him off and threw my bags on the bus and got on, the lad was swearing his head off at me and hurling stones at the bus. Bill thought it was risky to argue with these types as did Arthur the driver, he had two machine guns in a rack by his seat a pistol 9mm Browning on his belt,

"So are we getting issued guns then,"

I joked to the driver, he laughed,

"no, you might shoot yourself" he laughed.

The drive to the Shell compound took an hour as we passed through the very busy streets, I could see the abject poverty had not changed one little bit since my last trip here. People live in sheds that can only be described as a patchwork of wood and corrugated metal there is no pavements, just a dirt track worse still when it rains the filthy red water flows straight through the shanty town floods the sheds, bringing snakes and rats and sewage with it, in contrast, most of them have a satellite dish attached. We travelled at walking pace in our bullet proof MPV Bill aimed his camera at the appalling conditions a couple of locals ran at the bus Bill jumped back in shock,

"hey man don t let these people see you taking pictures, they hate it they're not proud of their lives," shouted the driver.

"Nigerians are not daft, we know the sweet blessed life you westerners live you can't blame them they never asked to be born a Nigerian, a murder takes place here every few minutes, life is cheap here, so you better remember that."

Bill was shaken by the hostile attack; the assailants had left their spit and saliva all over the window. I must admit I was shocked too; thus, Westerners always have bodyguards. It was very hot and humid the sweat was running down my face.

"what is that smell"! Bill exclaimed

"rotting flesh there must be a dead body nearby whether it's a human or animal who knows," laughed the driver.

The smell was making us nauseous we stopped at the traffic lights there it was a dried up human corpse laying half way on the road his legs flattened by the traffic insects completely covered the body it must have been there some time the smell of the decay was so strong I nearly threw up.

"You will see more of that before you leave,"

128

laughed Arthur (the driver)

"It's a common site, we have no real police force we live in anarchy no infrastructure to control anything like garbage, there is no system, so it builds up in huge piles like that one there,"

he pointed out I could see women and children searching through it for food or anything of value. What a way to live when you consider these people are very religious! What a tragedy clearly Religion has not helped them. It brought me back to my last visit so I promised myself this time will be different.

"We are coming up to the security gate, so you need to have your ID ready there are two gates, you need it for both, this is the only real safe haven for you white guys, you would not last 5 minutes outside of here believe me."

I believed him survival of the fittest is the only way here. It makes you realise how lucky we westerners are, if the local mafia or thugs don t get you the diseases will, if you get sick you die, no NHS here! Surely it must have reached tipping point by now, to bring this country to some kind of order would be an immense project. It's a culture developed over years of corruption and tribal wars, worse part of it is that the women and children that suffer the most.

The Shell compound was well looked after it looked just like the British army camps, I spent my wild childhood in. White painted stones lined the roads and small driveways leading up to the small flat roofed bungalows, the grass was cut short, hedges bordered the lawns roses adorned the walkways all very neat a far cry from the chaos outside the camp walls Billy spotted the full size pool,

"that'll do me Mike" Bill chimed

"I'll be writing the reports sat by the bar you can go on tour around the rigs" he laughed he was serious. We checked in at the reception which reminded me of a Military guard house a large room no pictures on the walls just white paint with an army green border 6 "wide right the way around the room and shiny polished floors, just a small desk with a very old computer perched between two young girls ready to take us round to our rooms. Mine was next door to the reception Bills was at the far end of the building. My room was really big a double bed and chest of drawers, TV, and fridge which was not working it all looked lost in the very large room. Opposite the door were large patio doors leading onto a grassed area we were told not to open them unless we wanted to be invaded with insects and rodents or even snakes. The bathroom was really basic apart from the drain smell and the very large cockroach in the empty bath. I unpacked my stuff and found a large bar of chocolate lying in bottom of my bag, it was all soft Karen must have slipped it in. I nipped to reception I asked Alice, the receptionist to put it in her fridge she promised to get mine fixed.

"you can eat at the pool club at 8pm it's quite good you know"
she smiled.

She was a pretty girl it must so very difficult for a young woman living in this hell I bet she felt privileged to be working here, the alternative did not bare thinking about. I recalled the girl I met on my first trip to Nigeria she had considered herself well off as a prostitute for the ex-pats after her parents had sold her to the local gangsters.

"Come on Mike let's go eat stop chatting up that lovely girl she's too young for you,"
Bill laughed,
"I am a woman not a girl," Alice chuckled,"
Nigerian women normally marry older men, the young men have no means of supporting a family unless they work for the local Mafia, life expectancy for those men was very short if you were at the bottom of the pecking order.

We looked around the pool and restaurant it was great again a mirror image of the club you find on British military camps abroad I was used too.

"This is gonna be a great job, Bill, we should try to spin it out we'll plan out our work, so we spend most of our time here what you think?"
"Oh yes, you bet, well I will be,"
Bill quipped,
"in any case I write a better report than you Mike, I've heard all about your escapades you must be used to trouble Mike, so you go and collect the info and pictures from the rigs and spend every other day here."

Bill knew I would not mind my wild side would not allow me to sit by the pool all day, we joined the Nigerians at the buffet I laughed as Bill could not identify one single dish,
"dam" he swore under his breath,
one of the waiters saw his disappointment,
"Sir, I can get you a cheeseburger with chips if you prefer,"
"now you're talking my good man make it two please and two cokes."

The waiter rushed off we seated ourselves in great anticipation we had not eaten since we left Paris 8 hours earlier the food on the air France flight was poor.

The morning greeted me with a chorus of birds singing as the sun shone through the lace curtains, I had a good feeling about this job, (I was soon to regret that thought). Bill and I sat down to breakfast toast boiled eggs the usual Brit Breakfast. A call from Colonel Omni he had arranged my schedule for the week, Bill refused to set foot outside the camp. The first job was at a swamp barge in the delta a very dangerous area for expats the rebels frequently attacked rigs and took hostages. I was to spend 3 maybe 5 days there. The ten-armed soldiers picked me up at 10 am prompt we left the safety of the camp. The site that greets you as you join the busy throngs of people rushing through the filthy streets, on mopeds and Honda cg125 motorbikes, all swerving to avoid the many deep holes in the road most of the people on board the little Honda 125 motorcycles often was 3 or 4 people to one bike, the traffic is so chaotic we never exceeded walking pace, I could see how easy it must be to stop a car and drag a hostage out, a chase would be or most impossible, so I sat in the back with a soldier either side of me, memories of my last trip here came flooding back I pressed myself low in the seat. I was instructed to put my seat belt on it because it made it that bit more difficult for a rebel to drag me out the car! The jeep convoy stopped at a clearing outside the bustling town, a chopper hovering 50 feet above the grass came down as we approached, the sergeant beckoned me to board the chopper I grabbed my bag and scrambled on board, as I strapped myself in we climbed skywards which made the seat belt fastening so much more difficult, they were taking no chances on me becoming the next hostage. For the next 2 hours I could only see jungle and the occasional canoe travelling through the swamp waterways. These people were still living as they had for generations the canoes were dugouts the spear shaped paddles doubled as a weapon later in the trip, I witnessed the tribal women trading sex for fresh water

Dugout canoe

I could see the swamp barge number 27 in the distance as we circled it for a few minutes it was normal practice just check there were no rebels around. Two fast zodiacs speed along the tributaries they were heavily armed with a very large machine gun fixed at the bow, both soldiers held machine guns as the chopper descended. I could see the hand grenades hanging from their shoulders, I remembered my thoughts earlier about the trip maybe I was wrong about this being a good trip what the fuck was I getting into. The touchdown had my two bodyguards leap out and take up a kneeling position at the edge of the helideck. With great trepidation I climbed off the chopper I was meet by the Tool pusher a black Nigerian his big toothy grin or most dazzled me.

"Hi mister Mike welcome to my rig lets go inside before you are

spotted by a sniper."

A hot flush ran down my spine as he said that, I considered asking to get back on the chopper.

As the chopper disappeared I had a feeling of great dread and loneliness, I followed him into the accommodation it was dark and depressing, the whole place painted the same colour of light green the corridors were narrow, barely wide enough for one person, It seems that this is normal it is harder to fight in confined spaces the pusher informed me which scared me even more as he pointed out the bullet impacts from previous attacks, there was hatches that dropped over the stair wells, it seemed to me they must of had a number of attacks.

"Call me Chris, Mike we all get along fine here it's all easy going but I must run you through the procedure of what you must do when the rebels attack, it happens quite regularly, we have a safe room all the ex-pats lock themselves in,"

"ok Chris your scaring me now I can see you must have had regular attacks maybe I should leave now,"

Chris laughed, "you're a funny man Mike just try stay inside so they can't see you from the jungle,"

That sounded familiar.

I could see all the small round dents in the metal walls from the bullets one watertight door was completely bent as was the frame Chris noticed me looking,

"that was a hand grenade, Mike, in fact, that was the room your expat lot used to hide in, but we have built a much stronger one now."
he laughed,

We passed through the corridors into the galley it was much the same the walls peppered with bullet holes and dents. Chris handed me a coffee.

"let's eat Mike just help yourself, the burger was crap, but I ate it, Chris seemed so proud of his rig and the food. A tall bald white expat came in,

"Hi, my names Miles I am the rig Electrician, I hear you're an ex Rig Mechanic, I'll show you around then you could start your survey tomorrow."

"Great where am I bunking then,"

"You can share with me If you don t mind the top bunk."

We scurried along the narrow dark corridors, then Miles pulled out his keys unlocked the cabin door and looked very serious,

"I keep it locked because these lot will steal anything so be warned Mike, I'll get you a key."

The cabin was dark and eerie just like the rest of the place, I looked at the bathroom, it was just what you would find in the average caravan very small and functional. I tossed my bag on the top bunk pulled out my notepad and camera.

"ok Miles let's get started, I want be out of here real sharp like, so I 'll begin checking over the rig now."

133

Miles Laughed "don t worry about the rebels I've been hostage once they just took me upriver it took a few hours to their camp and let me have freedom of the camp for 3 days then once Shell paid up, I was brought back to the rig."

"You must have been terrified"

"Not really"

"fuck off you must have been scared anyone would have been unless you're crazy of course you have returned here afterwards so perhaps you are crazy."

I laughed.

I spent the next couple of days inspecting the rig, I must say the local lads were a great help showing me around. Each evening I sat with them at the rear of the rig bullshitting and watching the jungle wildlife, some of the lads were hunting using Falcons, amazing to watch, around the bend in the river was a small barge where the 4 security guards lived, mean looking bunch. One evening a canoe approached it had two women occupants they had a large plastic drum placed between them in the canoe, two of the guards intercepted them.

"they have come to trade for clean water Mike"

Sammy the roughneck laughed.

"watch and see" he chuckled,

sure enough the women were escorted to the embankment in our view, the exchange began with both women bent over a fallen tree allowing the guards to shag them doggy style, this lasted about ten minutes before the rig crew started the applause the guards were not amused and raised their guns before pulling up their pants, we all scattered I peeked back around the corner they were laughing, so we all resumed our ringside seats. The women got their water and left.

"Hey, Mike, you fancy a go with them I will call them back"

Sammy laughed.

"Who the guards or the women" I joked.

Chris suddenly appeared,

"Hey Mike, you and the other ex-pats must leave ASAP I have word the rebels are coming soon."

"Fuck", I was shocked to my core my hand started to tremble,

"why me it's always me it's that fucking Grim Reaper again, when?"

I croaked.

"Maybe a few hours a chopper will be here in an hour it will have two escort choppers with it."

134

I rushed to the cabin and threw all my stuff in my bag like a crazy person, Miles came in,

"Mike its ok they won't hurt us long as we don t resist,"

"easy for you to say how do you know they are not the same rebels that took you,"

Miles stopped and thought

"you have a point," he started packing

I could hear the throbbing of a chopper engine approaching relief washed over me saved I thought, too late! It was followed by the rattle of machine gun fire; fuck I felt the colour drain from my face.

"Mike Miles get up here the choppers waiting,"

Chris screamed,

boy I have never moved as fast as that moment I ran through the narrow dark corridors up the stairs into the blazing sunlight which dazzled me for moment, I could see the chopper hovering a few feet above the deck, I could hear the gunfire over the sound of the chopper I kept running, I could feel Miles right behind me, bullets hit the deck to the side of me my legs or most gave way beneath me as I swerved to avoid them I dived on to the chopper Miles landed at the same time crushing me beneath him, the chopper raced skywards and forward at such an angle that we both slide down toward the pilots seats, the chopper was skimming the tops of the trees.

"Made it" I said relieved in a trembling voice

"don't speak too soon," the pilot shouted,

"we may have been hit, our escort is right behind us these rebels have ground to air missiles so we not out of it yet, this lot are not the usual rebels this lot seem more intent on shooting us down one of you two must be important to them."

Can't be me I was thinking.

My hands and legs were still trembling clearly, I was in shock. I watched Miles he was very quiet his hands were covered with blood he looked very pale, blood covered the floor, I could see a hole in his neck, blood was flowing out of it I pulled off my shirt and tried to stop the blood but he died just before we landed!

Once we landed the chopper was met by more soldiers and medics, they rushed Miles away, I could see a few bullet holes in the side of our chopper one of the escort choppers was smoking quite badly, there were some tree branches jammed in our choppers undercarriage, some of the pilots were shouting at each other. Once I had calmed down a car arrived and took me back to the compound, I could see Bill waiting by reception he looked very worried I walked up to him.

"so much for a good trip" I said my voice was shaky my hands and knees trembled.

He laughed "you're ok then, shit Mike I am glad I never came,"

Alice hugged me, she told me she heard on the radio your chopper was involved in a shoot-out at rig 27, three locals were shot dead on board the rig and two ex-pats made a miraculous escape through a firefight and two choppers were damaged,

"you must rest Mike you will be in shock; I will make you hot drinks I will take you to your room come now or you will fall you are trembling all over."

Bill put his hand on my shoulder,

"fuck Mike lets go home, fuck this place."

Alice took me to my room and ran a hot bath,

"Mike the bath is ready for you, when I return you better be in it,"
she laughed.

I stripped off as I stepped into the bathroom, I saw myself in the long mirror, I had blood spattered all over my face and down my neck, I walked back and looked at my clothes which were also covered in blood. I didn't notice it before although I was in bit of daze, dizziness overcame me, I hit the hard-tiled floor, I opened my eyes to see Alice and Bill staring down at me,

"Mike, Mike can you her me?"

"yes, Bill I can, why is my head pounding shit it hurts," I mumbled,

"Mike, we found you lying on the floor half an hour ago you must have blacked out the Doctor is on his way so you must stay in bed,"

"I will make sure you do, you are a menace Mike Bill has told of your reputation," Alice chuckled.

Bill laughed, "sounds to me like you're in luck Mike,"

I fell asleep shortly after, the last thing I heard was Alice telling me about how she got her job, I awoke to find Alice lying next to me, the moon light was bright shining through the lace curtains. I spotted a pile of clothes at the bottom of the bed, they were not mine Alice had stripped off, I looked under the sheets she was naked my mind raced,

"Like what you see Mike, I do,"

"Of course, you are very beautiful Alice,"

"I was, but he was killed two years ago we have no children I am only 25, so I have plenty of time to find the right man,"

136

"do you have any boyfriends just now,"
I had to keep talking to take my mind off the erection growing bigger every second. Alice fell asleep I dreaded falling asleep in case I had a bad dream I watched her sleep the long black hair covering her boobs the narrow waist, she was so black she was or most blue, her large brown eyes were haunting, her features were fine or most of European extract. Her voice sounded gravely large breasts an hourglass figure. She woke up.

"Mike what am I seeing there?" Pointing at the lump in the sheets, she smiled,

I smiled back,

"Alice I am in bed with a naked beautiful woman what would you expect?"

"That is what I was expecting Mike that is why I stripped off,"

she leant over and kissed me. Several times that night my mind ran wild what could have happened if the rebels got us, I woke up in a cold sweat Alice calmed me down.

My hand trembles had calmed a bit by the time I woke up in the morning Bill was banging on the door.

"Mike Breakfast mate you feel any better you will with some food in you."

later that day we received instructions to take a few more days off and chill by the pool. The more I thought about the trip to rig 27 the more I was amazed I got through it. I had a call from Chris the pusher he was really upset about the 3 lads that were shot on the rig.

"Mike those boys were on the helideck with you we were astounded that you ran right through the gunfire, we all heard you are a crazy fucker, we think you must be blessed. I expected you to run back to the accommodation, but you just kept running, did you know Miles was holding on to the back of your shirt as you ran,"

now the bad news,"

"Bad news how can there be bad news after that lot."

I exclaimed,"

"When you and Miles leapt on to the chopper his back was covered in blood I think he was hit in the neck while running across the helideck, you were probably still in shock to notice, so you came as close as you 'll ever get to being shot someone is watching over you Mike. We are all pleased you are fine; will you be returning to finish the report."

I laughed,

"of course, sometime in the next 50 years maybe,"

"I'll email you for any information I need to finish it how's that, has Miles family been informed?"

"he had no family Mike,"

"how utterly sad is that Chris, will he be flown home?"

Bill and I finished off the report a week later, during which I had a call from a somewhat irritated Colonel Omni.

"Mike, did you know that Bill, has insulted me, I am very angry too, do you think I am doing a bad job of Your security, Bill thinks it is my incompetence that you were involved in the shooting at the rig and that I should have known the rebels were coming there."

What could I say, Bill was right, but if we ever wanted to go home, I thought it best to keep the Colonel sweet?

"Colonel, I am sure Bill was just upset, I think he feels he should have been there too, also he recently lost his wife to Cancer,"

"Mike, he should have been there, that was part of his job why did he not go,"

"Bill writes a better report than I do so I made deal with him that he writes the report while I gather information, in any case if he had been there you may have had two deaths, but I am happy with our security, I will talk to Bill for you and I will ask him not make his opinion known to others."

"Thank you, Mike, I will be most happy if you do. I spoke to the shell office today, I believe they will be asking you to look at a land rig belonging to KCA, it is moving to an area called Ggoko it is a long drive through the wilder side of my Country, it is a dangerous place Mike, I know I should not be asking you to go after the last incident, I have asked KCA to forward you all the rig information they have so you will not have to stay very long, perhaps 4 hours, you will have 16 soldiers with you and you will be issued with a fire arm, take some days off to recuperate, I think Shell will contact you in the next week, but don't let Bill speak to them please."

Sounded to me like he was in fear of losing his job.

"I'll wait for the call Colonel but remember a favour for a favour I joked."

I discussed it with Bill he made it quite clear he hated the colonel and there was no way on Gods earth, he was going on the trip, he tried to persuade me not to go, telling me I was crazy so did Alice.

"Mike you are a stupid man if you go, I am sorry, but you may not return, even I would not go there, why would you go? Do you have a death wish those tribes still have spears and loin clothes? Death means nothing to them please don't go."

She walked left slamming the door.

I called the office Mark gave me the choice to go or not but offered me a bonus if I did go.

"Bonus Mark what does that mean?"

"He stuttered,

"well let me speak with Shell, I know all the rig sections have not arrived on the site yet, its gonna be a wild cat well so there's plenty of time, in fact I'll ask them to send someone to go and check out the area to make sure it safe."

It occurred to me they must be desperate to get approval for this rig to work there.

"Ok Mark let me know once it's been checked out."

Being a sucker or as Alice put it an idiot, I agreed to go, it still filled me with sense of dread, 4 jeeps 16 soldiers did not fill me with confidence. Colonel Omini, assured me he had every possibility covered I doubted that, even though the area had been checked for any recent incidents or Native unrest. It seemed to me the rebels, by all accounts were well organised and seemed to outmanoeuvre the powers that be quite regularly. Alice heard I had agreed to go on the trip and tried to persuade me not to go again, later, I heard her arguing with the corporal who came every day to check on us, she told Bill the Corporal had told her, he did not think they could guarantee my safety, so she tried to get them to cancel the trip, I called Chris at rig 25, he thought it would ok he had not heard of any recent incidents there for a while although it did once have a reputation for violence, but not recently. Next morning 6 am the convoy arrived one of the land rovers had a very large machine gun mounted at the back belts of ammunition draped down either side, the soldier who stood behind it looked like a nutter a very large man well over 6'6" a face well scared, snake like eyes he smiled at me revealing a mouth devoid of teeth bar one at the front, a huge scar ran from his forehead down to his neck it must be an inch thick.

Alice nudged me,

"Mike don't stare at him he is a mad man I have heard of him he loves his job, if there is trouble Mike, you must stay close to him."

Bill concurred "Jesus Mike I am not sure who's scarier him or the rebels."

I had to sit in the back a soldier either side of me the corporal handed me a nine-millimetre browning pistol,

"you know how to use this" he smiled.

"I certainly do I was using these when I was a young lad in Malaya back in the 60's,

I spent my school holidays cleaning up at the Army shooting range in Malaya, the soldiers taught me how to shoot.

He stuffed it back in the holster, I fastened it to my shoulder, why did I get the feeling I was about to jump out of the frying pan into a big fire. the corporal told Bill,

"We should be back sometime tonight."

He leapt into his jeep off we drove down toward the security gates I really felt like jumping out now and hiding in my room. I called the colonel he assured me no one would try anything with these soldiers because they were his personal bodyguards and very good at their job. "so don t worry Mike you will be fine but you will need to get all your information today this is the only chance you will get because I will need my men back tomorrow for another job and stay off the phone least don t tell anyone where you are going over the phone."

That had me speechless why not, I thought do these rebels have the capability to monitor Mobil phones!

As we passed through the shanty towns our convoy brought a lot of attention, I could see the mess in the streets, young children in rags, no shoe's, sores covered their faces and feet. We had to travel slowly through the villages, kids were clearly malnourished, flies swarmed around their eyes, the children were so used to it they just left them to lay their fly larva in their eyes, rats scurried about within inches of the children, in fact, the rats and humans were in competition to find food, amongst the garbage. Life expectancy must be short here even shorter if you get shot. The young kids even carried a gun of some sort. Further along, as we cruised along the riverbank, I watched the women washing clothes on the banks, not a few yards away was a toilet perched at the end of a small rickety jetty sticking out over the river.

Our small convoy cleared the town and we sped up into the wilderness it was nothing but jungle, the road was full of huge holes, many times we had to turned off the road to get around the bigger ones which looked a lot like bomb craters, we used a small track through the thick jungle to get around them, twice I had lizards and insects running over my shoulders making me jump, my travel companions thought it funny. After 3 hours traffic of any sort was very scarce, the road became narrower the jungle had thinned out, the road had become a track the convoy was now even slower not much more than walking pace, the odd Nigerian stood at the roadside to let us pass I was told to get lower down in my seat, I could see their tribal markings this was a number of scars on the neck or the cheek depending which tribe they were from, the scars were just lines perhaps 3 inches long but thick so they were easily seen, We arrived at the rig about lunch time the rig was in a compound surrounded by a 20ft wall built with Breach Blocks, erected solely for this well. Soldiers guarded the high gates, they were heavily armed, the convoy had to nose its way through the local tribesmen who deliberately blocked our way, they looked just like Natives they still carried their spears and wore loincloths. They lined the track as we passed, Machetes and gun barrels were scraped along the windows of my jeep, of course, I was terrified I sank down low in to my seat hoping they couldn't see me, I was bracing myself ready for the first shot, I anticipated was to come at any moment, I had never been that close to the wrong end of an AK 47. I suddenly realised if they were to shoot me no one would be there to arrest them my body would be dumped in the jungle, Nigeria has no law it is anarchy, the price of life and death could be the price of a good meal for the assassin. As the gates opened the guards aimed their guns at the natives so they wouldn't rush the gate, the convoy drove in, the rig was in sections that will make my job so much easier. I got out and looked around the entire compound it was the size of a football pitch, there was a gun post at each corner, barbed wire ran in several rows above the brick walls, I saw one guard with a rather large nasty looking Dobermann Pincher. "I'll be avoiding him" I thought.

I was thirsty and very hungry the aroma of food was too much; I could see the smoke from the cook house. I made a bee line for it; several caravans formed a circle, at the centre stood a round table complete with umbrella.

"Hey white boy come and eat if you dare,"

laughed this very black bald hard as fuck looking bloke,

"come and site eat, your name is Mike yeah,"

I held out my hand,

"and you are"?

"Abdul, come and eat."

I sat as ordered there on the table was a real tasty looking prawn salad with chips a cool beer, I savoured every mouth full.

"Delicious excellent who made this? way out here in this hot humid wilderness and you have food this good, you must have a good cook," Abdul called out,

"hey Boris, come out here you have an admirer."

A very tall man about 7-foot-tall walked out into the blazing heat, he looked so skinny my first thought was hell he must have a problem finding clothes to fit him, he had a pale complexion long black hair. He looked in my direction,

"fuck this I not staying out here long it's too hot,"

He looked at me,

"what the fuck you want pal?"

"err nothing I thought your salad was very good,"

"so, fucking what,"

he stomped back into the air-conditioned trailer,

"miserable fucker" Abdul laughed.

Fortunately the survey went smoothly, it was getting dark as we left the compound, my body guards were on high alert as if expecting trouble, so I sank down in my seat, I fell asleep for a while when I woke up it was pouring with rain and it was very dark no lighting of any sort just the light from our jeeps. We got back to the compound late that night, the office light was on it was nearly midnight. I was a bit peckish I remembered the chocolate I left in the office fridge. I knocked, Alice opened the door,

"working late Alice?"

"I'm just waiting to see if you came back safely Mike,"

By the look on her face I knew she was serious,

"we did not think you would, there has been news today,

"there is a dispute between the two tribes over which one will be assisting the drilling rig the rebels have stirred them up, we were told not to phone you in case the rebels got wind of it"

Alice was clearly very upset,

"It went ok the worst part was the drive up there and back but thank you for your concern"

"I am very sorry Mike, but I have eaten your chocolate while I was waiting for you" I laughed

142

"you will need to pay a penalty for that,"
she looked horrified,
"I am joking Alice it gives me the shits anyway any chance of a coffee?"
She laughed "ok Mike I'll bring it to your room you go shower it will be the best coffee you have ever had,"
After the shower Alice arrived with two coffees, she sat on the bed with me.
I saw Bill at breakfast,
"I hear it went well so what time did you get back?"
"I v got everything we need for the report, the best thing they can do with that rig is scrap it, the foods good though I 'll be taking few days off while you write the report."
"It's ok for you, the only food I can eat is cheeseburger or Bolognese try that for 2 weeks, I dread going to eat now, each meal is the same I'm sick of it I need to go home."
"we will be, soon won't we?"
"Ah! Bit bad news buddy"
my heart sank, "what now?"
"There's a Shell swamp barge it's been stacked at Kidney Island harbour for the last 5 years, they need to know its condition, basically is it worth doing up? There's a catch though but there is a bonus again."
"A bonus, why is it dangerous?"
Bill thought about it for a minute,
"you better ask Omini, I for one am not going there, Mike and neither should you,"
"it can't be worse than the last two trips surely,"
"you wanna bet, the head waiter at the pool told me about Kidney Island, his father was shot there just last week, in fact access to the dock is through a very violent shanty town. That's a risk in itself, anyway, speak to Omini, or the head waiter, I am calling the office, no one told us this trip would be so dangerous, I think we should get more money."
Bill was well pissed off, I think mainly because he had never ventured out of the shell secure compound, he felt he had let me down although he had done a great job of the reports much better than I would have.
Alice arrived at the pool early one morning along with colonel Omini he was in uniform. This must be official I thought Omini looked angry

143

she quickly and curtly introduced him then marched off. Millie her assistant was a few steps behind him, she made a comment to him I wasn't in ear shot. The colonel snapped at her as she ran off, "cheeky little bitch he said I 'll punish her for that, female labour is cheap she will be on the street by tomorrow."
I was out raged,
"Colonel I hope not, or you and I will no longer be friends"
I said,
"she has been very good to us and has made us very welcome to Nigeria,"
"I am just annoyed; does she think I want to send you guys out to these dangerous places. I am under pressure you know, if you get shot Mike I will be sacked or demoted,"
I laughed is that all your worried about, your job,"
"Of course, not Mike, but if it were not for the oil companies Nigeria would still be in dugout canoes and mud huts people here don't remember that.
"I need to keep them happy, so they will invest here and create jobs, I will give you my personal guard like the last time, but yes it is dangerous, there the snipers take shots from across the river in the jungle, I will send three gun boats to patrol the river before you get there, they will stay during your visit but you must try and keep a guard between you and the jungle all the time. I will also supply you with food for the day you can only go there once," "Err why only the one time?"
"they will spot you if you go back, they will be waiting with a sniper."
I was stunned, "So why are we going at all, just get the locals to tow the rig to a safer location,"
"Shell are worried it will sink,"
"If that is the case then why not just scrap it?"
"And we can go home."

"Not that easy Mike there's a lot of equipment inside the vessel like the engines, generators Draw works, pumps all worth millions plus all the certification plus all the rest of the red tape, someone has to go."
I'd hoped he hadn't thought of that.
Bill was right of course I knew it had to be me. The Colonel stared at me in a moment of silence, expecting me to give him my answer.

The Corporal who had been with me throughout the last trip, stood behind the Colonel nodding and smiling, he broke the frosty atmosphere,

"Mike you will be ok, I will be with you all the time the local tribe on the island are frightened of me and my men, when they see it's me they will keep away, but we must go soon before news of the trip gets through to the locals, it always does sooner or later."

I decided to go, the Colonel was clearly delighted it would reflect well on him and his squad of militarised thugs.

"You can hang on to the pistol we gave you just remember to give
 It back before you leave," laughed the Corporal.

 I felt quite safe with the pistol strapped to my chest it felt kind of comforting, I grabbed my backpack,
"ok let's go you coming too Bill" I quipped,
 Alice shouted at me,
"Mike you are a stupid fool it is a bad place the people that live in that area are terrorists."
The Colonel was on his phone right away,
the gunboats would meet us at the port.

Gun boat three.

Once our convoy reached Kidney Island we had to pass through the shanty town the streets which were more like dirt tracks, only just wide enough for the jeeps to pass at walking pace, the pot holes were so huge we were down to first gear, the locals pressed their faces against the windows shouting at the soldiers, they dragging their long Machetes along the windows grinning a big smile which sent a shiver down my spine, showing their rotten teeth. I decided to keep a low profile, so I pulled my hard hat down at the front to hide as much of my white face as possible. I could hear what sounded like the jeep getting a kicking my black colleagues hurled abuse back in what sounded like a jibe language. These people lived at the lowest level of poverty I have ever witnessed, the shanties (sheds) made up of bit of wood and corrugated iron no doors or windows. I could see inside; the floor was just soil or sand. Everyone dressed in rags, no shoes the children mal nourished sores all over their faces and feet, flies everywhere the smell was eye watering. My bodyguard told me the smell is rotting bodies of dogs and people rats and the odd horse, my first thought was I'm glad my hepatitis is up to date. Every time it rains heavy all this mud on the track gets washed away into the huts then into the harbour.

Once we reached the harbour and passed through the huge gates which had several soldiers on platforms raised above the track the gates shut behind us, I could see the swamp barge tied up to the harbour, across the river some 500 yards was the thick jungle. I could see a number of abandoned ships of different sizes marooned on the riverbanks. In the Jungle the Corporal told me the worst dregs of mankind,

"They will kill you for your shoes, Mike if they come across in boats, I will lock you in the jeep it is bullet proof."

Now I was shitting myself, a thought suddenly struck me, I felt I was living through one these movies whereby mankind is surviving in the aftermath of a nuclear war, there were wrecked ships stripped of anything useful, some ships were half submerged with people living on them. The water was a filthy grey colour a permanent smell of sewage dominated the entire area any wonder. I took a closer look the contents of the river drifting by was mostly sewage I nearly threw up.

"Hey Mike, you must stay behind the guards remember"

The Corporal ordered,

My two thugs looked round at me with a smirk.

"Bullets hurt Mike we've been shot before even just a nick hurts imagine a red poker rammed into your arm it burns like hell,"

Thug Number 1 showed me all his scares there must have been 10 maybe more all large and messy, he was an ugly bugger too, the largest of his scars was the 4 inch one that ran from one cheek to the other passing through the dent in his nose,

"Machete" he said.

"What happened to the other guy?"

"he is dead so is his mate,"

I had completed most of the survey of anything worth saving like the engines, what was left of them the rebels had cut a huge hole in the side of the vessel and taken whatever they could, the accommodation! It was stinking to high hell it took my breath away, the galley was crawling with every insect and fungi on Gods earth, I darted out into the blazing sunshine it blinded me for a minute or two. I turned back to shield my eyes I shaded my eyes and walked slowly around the rusting containers on deck there was a dinging noise every few minutes.

Thug 1 was right behind me he grabbed me and pushed me down on to the deck between some containers,

"what the hell is that" I shouted,

thug 2 bent down picked up a bullet dropped it in my hand it was red hot,

"the rebels are here Mr Mike, and they are shooting at us, but they're hitting the steel work trying to scare you, Mike,"

Then the unmistakable rattle of machine gun fire had me terrified as I looked up, I could see gun boat one, the crew were hiding behind the cabin I hoped no one could see me hiding behind a rusty old container, I managed to take the pictures below.

Boat one. (The shooting incident)

Gun Boat no 2

The gunboats returned fire wildly into the jungle for a few minutes, then the rebels fired back, I laid there for what seemed like hours waiting for a break in the gun fire, finally it ceased I was trembling with fear my two thugs turned up out of nowhere picked me up.
"Home time Mike we need to leave now run those bastards know you are here they must have spotted your white lily face."

We left in a hurry once back at the compound Colonel Omini meet us at the compound gate with a big smile he laughed,
"Mr Mike I am so glad you are ok, one day your luck will run out I think the "Grim Reaper," he is watching you, I think you must stay in the Base from now on, come I have good brandy it will help your trembling hands."
 The Brandy calmed me down enough to explain to Bill and Alice what happened Alice was furious,
"Mike you are a fool your wife must be in bits,"

148

I interrupted her with a shout,

"I know my luck will run out,"

Bill shouted, "hey Mike she didn't deserve that, I was worried too, you are a fool, this is my first trip with you and I'm not sure I'll do another."

They were right,

"ok I'm sorry no more shouting, I never thought there would actually be shooting I've been in so many narrow escapes and came out ok so I probably think it will never happen to me I suppose, I have had a few people say to me the "Grim Reaper" is watching you "Mike" and I just laughed it off."

Bill looked at Alice,

"Alice don't go and speak to Omini, he will fire you for sure after we have gone, so keep quiet ok."

She gave me a dirty look and left.

He turned to me

"did you manage to get enough info for a report?"

"Yes I did and lots of pictures of the equipment on board the rig the decks are so rusty it's like walking over wafer biscuits, so it will need all the decks replacing, and the hand rails too, so we made up the report condemning the Rig since the rig could only be scrapped.

The resourcefulness of these people is amazing a large hole about 15 feet across had been cut in the hull the engines had been systematically dismantled and removed, the crankcases were all that was left, they were to big and heavy to move. Every part of the accommodation had been stripped bare. Mother Nature is relentless the steel decks were so rotten it was like walking over cream cracker biscuits, in fact, I'm sure if I'd tried, I could have put my foot through it. I often wonder if these super rich oil companies have become so big, they have lost track of their assets, on this occasion the company had paid to keep this rotten old rig berthed here for 5 years and forgotten about it. I have come across this on many occasions. Do they make so much money, these items don t matter, these rigs cost millions each, the average spec Jack up last time I checked in 1998 was about 45 million ready to drill? On a visit to the fiords in Norway in 1995, I saw 8 semi-submersible rigs stacked, they had been there over 5 years and just as rusty. this type of rig costs considerably more than the average jack-up rig. Such waste! We had to lay low for a week the colonel was concerned we may be snatched on the way to the airport. It had become quite a regular occurrence in Nigeria at that time for hostages to be snatch from cars, it was all well organised. We spent the week writing up the report by the side of the pool, the only thing we paid for was booze. One thing Bill had told me about the food although I had noticed the extent of our menu consisted of either cheeseburger or Bolognese after just 5 days, I hated it I tried the local food it made me quite sick. The remainder of trip went without incident Bill and I parted company at Charles de Gaulle airport. We said our goodbyes

"Mike I won't be coming with you again, you scared the shit out of me, what is it with you and trouble, I heard about your incident in Abu Dhabi you're a wild man, the Grim Reaper will get you sooner or later."

He laughed, shook my hand and disappeared through the gate.

Arriving home is always so great, I decided not to tell the whole story it would only worry them, I was now living with Karen in the 3-bed house I bought a few years earlier, after my ex-wife left us during the unpleasantness, the boys had lived with my mother, she supervised the boys moving us into the new house. While I was away the twins fetched the 8-ton van I had stored on a farm after I had driven it back from Spain with help of Sam my eldest son. The van contained all my belongings and furniture, I was honoured the large bedroom was mine. All our motorcycles were neatly parked in the garage. We enjoyed many runs out together the only problem was it started getting competitive, so I had to lay down some rules, but god knows what they got up to while I was away. The boys left the army when they returned from the Iraq war. They were so disappointed with the poor backup the Army received from the criminal Blair and his useless government. It was a long wait for the resettlement grants from the MOD which never materialised, so I had to pay for the courses which were a waste of time. There were no jobs after the courses because the courses were cheap it was Blair's pathetic effort to prop up failing industries.

A month later a call from Mark, he asked me and Karen over at his house which had me thinking, why? he's never done this before. The job was in Iran to overhaul a 400-ton sub-sea BOP,(Blow out preventer) at the time there were sanctions between the USA and Iran, so spares were sourced through Abu Dhabi, Mark spent £1.5 million on spares up front to show good will to the client the Iran government. This B O P (Blow out preventer) Was 5 years old and was never used because the rig it was intended for was not only a 20-year-old design it had taken 6 years to build it so the seals in the B O P, were past their shelf life and needed renewing. The job required 4 men, we were a man short Mark asked me if I knew anyone available,

"Only my son Samuel, he is offshore in Denmark Just now, but Ben, he's just out the Army, he was a Tank Mechanic during the Iraq war. He has never been offshore, but he is not scared of anything after that war, this will not scare Ben."

"It's risky Mike, what if we fall out with the Iranians, you could get stuck there if that's the case, Ben, will be handy as an ex-soldier fresh from war in the desert, best not tell the Iranians he is ex-soldier" I laughed.

"I'll watch out for him,"

"you mean he will watch out for you," laughed Mark.

Iranian Semi

My eldest son Sam was out working in the Danish sector, it makes a father so proud when he can be a help to his offspring start a new career. Sam was doing well, now I had the chance to help another son through another proud father Mark. Ben the wilder one of the boys jumped at it since he had been languishing at my house bored with life.

"it is so boring,"

he would often complain there must be something better than 9 to 5 crap every day the same."

I leapt through the lounge door like spider man,

"Ben" I shouted,

"I have your chance to get away from the humdrum of life and come with me to Iran to service a BOP."

A wide grin formed on his face,

"yeah dad sure, you should be taking Sam, I have not been offshore yet,"

151

"Sam is away just now and it's in the Sadra shipyard in Iran."
Matt is working, Tom is with his kids anyway this is your chance to make big money."
"so, what's the pay?"
"500 a day for a month,"
"you're having a laugh dad that would be amazing,
"No Ben that's it.
"I 'll pack," he rushed off upstairs.
"But we will need to go to London to organise visas."
Ben was clearly chuffed to fuck, at last, a job just like Dad and Sam, but Ben could now do something more challenging. Ben was really bright like his twin Matt. But wild like his brother Sam, Sam used to have to work hard at everything like me, but he never gave up, he always got there in the end but wild like the rest of us Youngman's it must be in the DNA.

What a horrible smelly place London is, and so busy, coming from the Scottish borders and the wide-Open spaces, this was a culture shock constantly Bumping into people was unavoidable, the noise and traffic were overwhelming. Within a week we were on our way to Iran, there was not much information about the actual job or about the meet and greet, so we all felt like we were on some adventure. Who knows anything could happen this time, relations with the west was not good there were not many ex-pats working in Iran at that time 2004, so we had to be very diplomatic? I could imagine the accommodation being some beat-up caravan at the dock side the toilet a stinking hole in ground. Ben and I had a good laugh about the possibilities, Ben, I could tell was really excited, a new adventure at last his life was moving on, plus he was earning good money, I was so grateful to Mark for giving Ben this chance. Tehran airport was not busy the rep met us at the arrivals which was a relief, we had no idea what to expect on this job two new cars were waiting at the exit, we loaded our luggage swiftly and we speed off, Ben and I in one, Scott and the Gary in the other car. Gary was the sub-sea specialist, Scott the safety expert both good men Scott I knew from past jobs he was great but a very quick temper, not a man to cross. I just hope the locals did not piss him off, he was a tough character. Scott took shit from no man, it was clear he and Gary were from different world's it was instant dislike from the outset Scott a tough switched on Scotsman, Gary an ex-university snob called himself the Doctor?? They had to share the car Scott was really

152

pissed off with me! Both cars set off winding through the chaos of the very busy noisy streets the driver, occasionally shouting at people he or most killed a few folk as he weaved around the pedestrians, no one seemed to care about the traffic, it seemed to blend in quite well our speed never managed to get past walking pace until we reached the motorway, which was no worse than the M25. After several miles, the driver answered his phone shouting at the caller we suddenly pulled over into the shade under a bridge narrowly missing another car parked there and standing there in the shade was Mark. We all looked at each other confused what the hell was he doing here? This was not in the plan he leapt into the car.

"Hi boys how was the flight?"

"Never mind that what's going on Mark you never told me you were coming this is all very cloak and dagger"

"There's been a complication, don't worry the jobs ok I just need to negotiate with the client, I spent 1.5 Million on spares for them, so I need to make sure I'm getting it all back, it's left me short of funds."

Alarm bells were ringing loudly in my head,

"shit am I gonna get paid, Ben will be well hacked off if we don't get paid,"

"Don t worry Mike I am not that broke."

Mark laughed as if reading my mind. It was a five-hour drive through what can only be described as desert and small villages, clearly the very poor are exploited by the rich bit like the UK. We passed by an army base it took a good few minutes to it was quite large but the vehicles and equipment I saw were at least 30 years old Ben commented,

"If they were to take on the west with that lot it'll be a walkover."

I was sat in the front we were on a road similar to our A roads the driver seemed to be suicidal, he was overtaking but there were other cars coming in the opposite direction, straight at us he swerved at the last possible second to avoid it, scaring us all this went on for a few miles before I decided to have a word with him but before I could I had to grab wheel and swing the car back in lane, the driver was not happy,

"Allah is watching over me"

he said in good English,

"Well he is not watching over me pal so stop this over taking crap,"

I told him,

Ben Laughed "you are a marked man now dad"

The driver smiled he understood.

"What is your name mate"

"Achmed, you English are not driving this way in the UK? then you know our Koran tells us when we die, we go to a better place, so we are not scared of dying,"

"ok then that's fine for you, but we are Christians our religion makes us no such promise so when we die there is only the unknown for us so we would like to stay in this world as long as possible mate."

He laughed "you should read the Koran, Mike, it will show you a better way of living."

Mark interrupted,

"Mike a word in your ear,"

he whispered, "don't get dragged into a religious discussion it 'll get us in trouble kill it now please,"

"We should stop for a piss soon what you think Achmed."

"We have a place coming up soon we will eat and have coffee there is toilet western type for you fellas."

Sure, enough we did stop, the locals were great we were treated like VIPs.

"so, where's this toilet then,"

Ben asked the owner of the café.

"it is down the alley next door please pay the doorman anything will do,"

I went along with Ben down the narrow ally a small scruffy old man sat at a desk an ancient Cadburys chocolate tin lay open on the desk, it had a few coins in it so we dropped a few more in it as we rounded the corner, the site that meets our eyes was so bad my eyes started smarting at the very strong stink of sewage, it was up the walls over the seats and on the floor Ben jumped back in horror,

"Fuck me!"

it was the toilet from the film trainspotting but worse

"Don't push me, dad, I might touch a wall or something I am not using this damn it I'm going to piss in the street."

I followed as Ben passed the old man, he grabbed his few coins and muttered to the old man,

"clean the fucking toilets you lazy bastard."

154

The old man laughed and nodded, of course, I had to laugh it was typical Ben. So, we did piss in the street but soon as Ben saw the owner, he walked straight up to him.

"hey mate have you ever use that toilet, its fucking disgusting clean it."

Ben stormed off and waited in the car, the locals were not amused at Ben's aggressive attitude, raised voices between the locals told me they were well pissed off, we all stared at each other waiting for an angry response from the Iranians (Farsi). Mark was worried I could see it on his face,

"Mike don't let Ben piss these people off, who knows what they'll do. It was hot now 40 plus at least, we were tired and pouring with sweat. We needed to get away from the heat Ben was in a mood.

Scott had been amused by the whole thing,

"hey Mike, this promises to be an amusing trip,"

he nodded towards Ben smiling.

"Ben does not suffer fools or take crap he tells it how he sees it; it could get us in a bind Mike shut him up please,"

Scott was right of course. The interpreter came over

"Mike we must leave, these people are feared of your son they say he has been blessed by Allah, the sign is the white patch of hair he has, I am not Sure what they will do I have told them we will leave and not bother them any longer so we must leave now."

As we were setting off, I looked back there was a policeman talking to the café owner and pointing at us as we drove off at speed. Now I was worried for Ben but I said nothing, I felt like kicking out the driver he was scowling at Ben through his rear view mirror, I was thinking I better sort this fella out in case he has a go at Ben if he did Ben would kill him.

"Don t worry Achmed I will punish my son when we arrive at the hotel, he should not have shown disrespect for the old man he is a guest here as we all are,"

He glanced at me, if looks could kill?

"Do you think I am stupid, Mr. Mike"

His response caught me wrong-footed, I never thought he was that intelligent. Mark asked him to pull over immediately he was on the phone I was not sure what was said but after a minute or two he handed the phone over to the driver. shortly after We were on our way again No one spoke for the rest of the trip. The hotel was situated in a little bay at the southernmost point of the Caspian Sea. There were no other guests the hotel was quite large it was modern too, it sat like a monument a mile from the Shipyard and 2 miles from what looked like a nuclear power station. We all had a room to Ourselves I made sure Ben's room was next to mine the rooms had no TV no nothing although they were nicely decorated, swimming was allowed in the bay. I was lucky enough to have a normal toilet everyone else had the Muslim type, a hole in the floor of course Ben asked me if he could use mine as he was anxious, he may shit into his pants as he squatted over the hole. He did go down to reception he asked for a room change for one with a real toilet, he told the receptionist why, he was informed you only drop your pants down to your knees then when you squat, that way you won't shit on to your pants. The atmosphere was lighter now we compared complaints then we all met later in the restaurant it was empty apart from us the food was based on raw cabbage and tomatoes the waiter came over and asked in broken English,

"Meat or Beef,"

we all laughed confusion was written over all the waiters face. A voice interrupted our laughter.

"I am Jerry the interpreter for you guys"

He chatted with the waiter; then waiter scurried off. Jerry smiled and sat down shook hands with us all, he then looked at me,

"You must be Mike I have heard about you from the driver I am told to watch out for you and your son he told me there was trouble on the drive here,"

"Yes" Mark put in,

"the two of them are trouble Scott will be keeping them out of trouble don't worry" Mark scowled at Scott.

He gave me dirty look. We were given a company car and driver to transport us each morning to the shipyard. The driver was pleased with himself what a cushy number hang around the yard all day until we were finished for the day, the car was a new Peugeot 405 bright yellow. A meeting was arranged with the Management of the yard and the rig owners who it seemed was the Iranian Government. I was sat next to Mark, Scott and the Dr Gary, who was scared of Scott, so he should be most people were, he did have a reputation for being abrupt and to the point, Ben sat in the corner he seemed highly amused by the whole thing, I knew what he was thinking it was best he kept his mouth shut at this time. Five of the Farcie sat opposite Mark the Farcie were dressed in their national dress except one, he was in jeans and tee shirt plus baseball cap a thin wiry type with snake-like eyes it was clear he was the man here, but laughter was on the cards when he spoke imagine an Iranian trying to speak with an American accent. Ben immediately excused himself to the loo to conceal his amusement. Mark and I kept a straight face as Sadra the owner spoke,

"I will be your point of contact while you are here anything you require; I will sort for you."

The phoney American accent was so funny, have you ever tried speaking while holding back laughter, you could imagine I had to look like I was as serious as he was, I could feel my face straining at the effort. I am sure he could tell by my clinched fists. Mark looked around at me my voice had jumped up an octave as I held back the urge to burst out laughing. I looked around the room the site of Scott with his head in his hands nearly did it I knew he was killing himself laughing, but Gary the Dr sat there straight faced he always looked that way, no emotion at all he just gave me a rather tiresome look like I am so bored with this. Mark was staring daggers at me.

"Mike answer the man,"

he whispered at me I needed to keep it short and end this meeting,

"l will let you know in due course when we have inspected the Rig and B O P, I will know how long the work will take, when can we expect our invoices paid, if you need copies of the invoices let me know."

The look on Marks' face was a picture to behold.

Sadra, looked surprised,

"Have they not been paid; I did not know, I will see to it tomorrow,

Mark was clearly surprised by my comments,

"Ok Mike, I think we will resume this meeting at a later time"

he scowled at me and walked out with Sadra.

A week later Mark had gone back to Aberdeen, Sadra had not been forthcoming paying Mark for all the Spares he bought on Sarda's word, I walked into the office, Sadra sat behind his huge antique desk,

"Sadra I have copies of the invoices from Mark, I thought maybe you had lost them since according to the contract they should have been paid long ago?"

Sadra looked up at me,

"Mike, I have it in hand, please do not worry"

he reminded me of a snake, the thin smile and small slit eyes, I noticed he never managed eye to eye contact for more than 2 Seconds which suggests a hidden agenda?"

all my years of traveling the world and dealing will corrupt officials had taught me to read people quite well.

"ok Sadra I will let Mark know he will receive payment in the next few days,"

Sadra stuttered,

"well maybe, Mike maybe longer,"

"oh, so it is not dealt with then, which is it?

I smiled,

"we have shown goodwill by purchasing your spares because the Americans will not deal with you, even though we had never met you before, Mark trusted you, so surely you must show us you can be trusted by showing us good will,"

"Ok, Mike I will show good will soon,"

I left, but unconvinced I called Mark and told him about the meeting,"

"Keep at him Mike, my company needs that money,"

Once back at the yard I explained the situation to the lads

"I 'll see him next Mike you're too soft man,"

I laughed, "and risk a war with these fuckers Scott, because you killed an official,"

Scott laughed, I could just imagine how that would go, pay up or suffer the wrath of Scott, ok Scott we'll be ready for world war three,

Ben laughed,

"can we listen at the door?"

 Ben chimed in.

It had been 3 weeks the work progressed ok.

Next morning none of the Iranian yard workers were nowhere to be found, after a look around the yard we heard that they had spent the night sleeping on the deck of the rig! Apparently, it was ready for sea, but the rig was far from complete let alone go to sea. The foreman was not happy once I convinced him of the fact.

"Allah is looking after us Mr. Mike, please don t worry,"

"that's good for you but not the rig So please keep your men off it just now or the god Neptune will take the rig and the men to the bottom of the ocean if it is not ready for sea."

I watched as he walked away a little confused, I could hear Ben and Scott laughing,

"your v got some nerve Mike, telling that shit to these poor unsuspecting people there will be some questions asked at the mosque tonight about the new God Neptune,"
we all laughed,
"Mike" it was Sadra,
"I have news my boss and owners of the yard will take you out for dinner Farcie style, we have a good restaurant up in the hills you will be collected from the hotel at seven,"
"thank you Sadra for a second there I thought you were going to tell me you had paid Mark."
He looked dejected he could see I was not impressed by the invitation we all three stared blankly at him for a minute he was clearly crestfallen.
"err ok boys see you later then,"
"maybe you slimy rat,"
Scott muttered in a deep Scottish accent this had Sadra really confused he scurried off it was clear Scott scared the shit out of him. This was not part of the plan as far as I knew, this was a rush job because the Iranians wanted their rig on location which happened to be on the border with Russia at the centre of the Caspian Sea. Ben thought we were being set up for assassination.
"it's what the Iraqi's did a few times during the war you must have pissed them off Dad."
"Mac the knife," Scott put in laughingly
"fuck off you guys I v not upset anyone yet,"
I laughed,
"I'll call Mark see what he knows."
It turned out he knew nothing of it.
The work was progressing well so it could not be that maybe it was their way of showing goodwill to divert us from the outstanding one and a half million dollars they owed Mark, I came to the conclusion that was it ,we were getting wound up over nothing. Sure enough, the cars picked us up at seven, I made sure I was in the same car as Ben, there were six cars two had armed soldiers one at the front the other at the rear. The route took us through quite number of villages, these people are very poor and poorly nourished. We stopped a number of times clearly the locals had not seen outsiders before they were amazed by Bens blonde hair, They spotted the white patch at the back

of his head, there was a lot of discussions and pointing Ben was getting concerned he was close to losing his cool, so I stepped in,

"Sadra what's the big deal,"

he smiled,

"The village elder is telling the people; Ben has been blessed by Allah!! the patch is where Allah touched him while in his mother's womb."

Is this coincidence? As mentioned earlier in this book a gypsy told me much the same thing!

I ushered Ben back to the car,

"People have told me that before, but it's just bullshit dad"

"so why don t you tell these people Allah doesn't exist then"

"very funny dad they would probably hang me or worse, its faith in Allah that keeps these people alive,"

That surprised me how astute for such a young man. An hour later up in the hills amongst the pine forests, we reached the restaurant it was or most dark now we were miles from anywhere, if this was an assassination this would be an ideal place my hands trembled as I got out the car I kept Ben close, Scott came over to be close too, I always felt safer with Scott close by,

"Get ready to run you two sod Gary he can kiss Iran arse."

We were herded into the building, one very large round table dominated the room four waiters stood to attention on the side-lines the four of us were split up to sit between the officials, Sadra sat opposite me the Iranians said a prayer with heads bowed Ben looked at me and rolled his eyes, Scott was smirking least the tension was gone I thought. After the prayers the waiters spun into action the first course arrived at my neighbours place it was a bowl of cold dark green soup there was the odd lump to be seen floating around in it, actually it looked like a bowl of snot as mine arrived I dare not let him place it in front of me lest I throw up, so I motioned him away before the snot came into my field of vision. I looked over at Ben to see the expression on his face, as he looked down at his bowl of green snot, I had to smother a laugh. Scott met my eye with a smile as he dared to taste the green slime the smile instantly vanished as the spoon came out of his mouth. The rest of the meal went by without incident until Sadra suddenly stood up.

"Attention please I would just like to welcome our western Engineers to our country it is good to know our rig will soon be ready to drill at sea the progress is good so far so we say thank you it is going to be a good relationship between us I am sure."

The Iranians all clapped my neighbour patted me on the back smiling he was too close his breath was stinking. I drew back as it took me by surprise, the man tried move closer as he spoke, I pushed him back,

"keep your distance pal"

I told him in a loud serious voice to emphasize my meaning he was not happy, a sudden silence took the room as everyone appeared to be staring at me it was this moment, I realised my arm was outstretched, it had a fist at the end of it! Scott was there in a flash grabbing my arm and folded it back, Sadra looked horrified as I stood up what could I say it was blatantly clear to all my intentions were to punch this man, who turned to be the Minister for the interior. I said the first thing that came to me,

"this man tried to kiss me, we do not do that in the UK it is a crime,"

Scott whispered, "you are a fucking liar"

"any suggestions then," I whispered.

The Minister started to laugh,

"but we do here Mike,"

in very good English Scott and I were shocked, we thought Sadra was the interpreter for them clearly not, no English had been spoken by any of these people Since we met them,

"what the fuck is going on, I Whispered to Scott?

I could see Gary shaking his head in disgust.

"We are very tired Sadra it has been a long hot day for us the long trip here has made us tired as well, maybe we should go, it is work as usual for us tomorrow."

A hurried discussion between Sadra and the officials took place in "Farsi" it was agreed we were excused one of the escort cars followed us back to the hotel, of course Ben and Scott tried winding me up.

"What were you saying about not pissing anybody off Mike, well you have really done it now," he paused, "this is not the route we came by," "you know what that means Dad,"

"no please tell me?"

"mac the knife mate," came Scott's reply.

"Very funny,"

I had to take this seriously Scott was a clever man, he knew his marbles he had a load of experience with these types of projects. I checked our route as we passed several landmarks, I had memorised on the way there we were ok it was the right route.

"how you gonna explain this to Mark, Mike, it was bad enough these folks not paying Mark, I would think it a lot less likely now, that you were gonna punch a minister dam?"

"We all want to be with you when you call him."

laughed Scott Ben joined in of course,

"you'll be fired, Dad."

We arrived back at the hotel near midnight. I left the boys at the lounge and went to bed, what the hell will I tell Mark? I could call him now it's not that late now in the UK my phone rang, it made me jump it was Mark my thoughts ran wild, had Sadra called him already, I v never been fired before, I picked it up and braced myself for the oncoming row.

"Mike how did the dinner go? Listen I've had a chat with the department of the interior of Iran, it seems the yard has just been put up for sale and all contracts have been suspended,"

"when was this?"

"Much earlier today."

"No one mentioned it here, we were told it is work, as usual tomorrow, Sadra didn't mention it at the morning conference today?"

Well, he should of I have a suspicion he is after brownie points,"

I explained the incident at the dinner, with the Minister, Mark burst out laughing, it was a good few minutes before he could speak.

"you should have punched him."

He chuckled,

"Tomorrow gather our stuff together anything important put it in the car enlighten the lads and wait until Sadra tells you the news if he does not call me."

I legged it down to the lounge they were all there to make sure we were not overheard I had to get them all alone perhaps my room.

"Listen you guys I v just had a chat with Mark I can't talk here some things a foot, come up to my room now."

I explained the conversation with Mark,

"that snake Sadra is up to something I know it" Ben went on

"I had a feeling about him,"

"yeah me to" Scott joined in, Gary said nothing which I thought a bit odd,

I said good night and went bed wondering what the next day had in the store, yet another exciting day.

I am sure just as most days turned out to be for me, ever since I came to work in the drilling industry way back in the seventies, my career has been full of exciting days filled with danger and uncertainty. I often found myself unsure if I would survive the rest of the day, surely the day will come when my luck will run out or my guardian angel will abandon me to the "Grim Reaper," I got little sleep that night, it occurred to me Gary had made no conversation concerning the incident or about Marks news or the money, he must realise the situation we could find ourselves in like getting held here to finish this job or even made to disappear once the BOP and rig are ready for sea surely not. I thought, one and half million dollars is nothing to Iran?? Maybe the Iran government has no knowledge of this operation, perhaps the department of the interior is acting alone with Sadra? We had our morning pre-job meeting with the yard foreman and our interpreter once out of earshot of Gary I told Scott and Ben of my suspicions regarding Gary.

"fuck off what could he possibly be up to out here?"

Scott laughed,

by lunch time there was no word from Sadra, I decided to go see him about the outstanding bills as I approached his office I spotted a pair of our company works boots outside the door, they must be Gary's I knew Scott and Ben were in the yard, the offices all had frosted glass sections I could make out Gary's tall lean figure, he was leaning over the desk I moved closer to hear them talking about money. I waited out of site until they left, Sadras name was on the glass door. I had a quick look inside through the letters covering the desk, under them were piles of money it covered the entire desktop, I moved away quietly was I seeing things?

I nipped back for another look; I was right first time I took a picture with my phone. Scott and Ben would not believe me, so I showed them the picture, I sat down with a cup of tea what the fuck was going on? Then it struck me that must be the money for Mark, but why is it cash? Ben stormed in.

"Dad we saw it, but Gary came out with his briefcase, so we followed him to the car He turned left outside the gate so he maybe going to the hotel, Scott has gone after him."

Sadra stood in the office doorway,

"Mike where is Scott going, I just saw him driving through the gates?"

"What the hell is going on Sadra, we know about the cash."

He was clearly shocked his mouth hung open for a few seconds he stuttered a few words,

"M, M, Mike you must understand if the yard closes, we will be without work or money, Gary has devised a way of filtering some cash from the project.

"Don t you mean stealing it from Mark, he knows if you people don't pay him there's nothing, he can do about it, but your government will think they have paid Mark or do they? or should I ask them."

I could see this was going to get nasty and I was digging us in deeper in over our heads Sadra could easily have us disappear.

Scott burst through the door with the minister and two security guards my first thoughts were for Ben shit what have I got us into now, but the guards grabbed Sadra handcuffed him and dragged him out.

"Mike" the Minister started.

I feared he was going to arrest us too.

"I have arranged for you three to get out, please go get your things use the car drive to Tehran, there are tickets waiting for you at the information desk, go now today, what trouble do you mean?"

I jumped to my feet,

he went on,

"the people who work here are from a faction different to the management, they are blaming the management for the shutting of the yard if the yard closes some of these people will starve Mike, it is not the same as in the UK, it is the government who is to blame there will be trouble, Sadra and Gary are taking advantage of the situation, but I have the money now I will give it to the yard workers I hope It will keep the peace Mike you must go now before it is too late."

I grabbed Ben and Scott we had to rush the minister sounded really worried he or most had me panicking.

"Do you think we will reach Tehran before trouble starts?"

Scott told me to stop panicking,

"we'll be fine although I am not so sure for Gary the thieving bastard".

The car sat outside the hotel it took us just minutes to get our gear and soon we were speeding to Tehran the trip went without incident. I was so relieved to reach home I felt so stupid for getting my son into such a dangerous situation. I started to worry about my other son Samuel who I had encouraged to work offshore a year previously to this. The following year I spent working in the North Sea as an ad hoc Mechanic it was possibly the most normal year I had ever worked.

On November 15th, 2009 4,30am I received the type of news that no parent should ever get! I was woken by Police pounding on my front door,
"I am sorry to inform you Mr. Youngman your son Samuel has been killed offshore in Demark"!
I nearly died that moment. Samuel had called me that night at 21.00 we had a long chat he was killed at 22, 15 through gross negligence this was the end of my life as I had known it. I was a changed person I pleaded to my local MP and Mr. Cameron for some influential assistance but the only reply I received was negative. I am sure it would have been different if it was his child. A succession of solicitors bleed every penny from me for the following year they made no progress so I fired them and continued alone I spent the following four years pursuing the three companies involved, I only worked the occasional job to pay my bills this effectively ended my career. The companies were eventually found guilty of breaking regulations and fined 10 million Euros each, but it was no comfort to the family. The grief of Losing a child never leaves you counselling was no use at all they gave up after 2 years. You just get better at concealing the constant feeling of grief. I have concluded that there is no god if there is this would not happen also how he dare allow this to happen, despite what is written in the bible.
"Suffer not, young children come unto me."
This is hypocrisy I have witnessed so much suffering during my career the possibility of a god is hard to believe unless he is a bad one who enjoys the suffering that is so rife in the world, no matter how much money is thrown at it there is no change. So, I say to those people who choose to believe in a god.

"Boy are you gonna be disappointed."

Love you Samuel.

Printed in Great Britain
by Amazon

51577663R00095